D0290786

Reprints of Economic Classics

THE ETHICAL AND ECONOMIC THEORIES OF ADAM SMITH

THE ETHICAL AND ECONOMIC THEORIES OF ADAM SMITH

BY

GLENN R. MORROW

[1923]

THE ADAM SMITH LIBRARY

REPRINTS OF ECONOMIC CLASSICS

AUGUSTUS M. KELLEY · PUBLISHERS

NEW YORK 1969

First Edition 1923
(New York: Longmans Green & Company, 1923)

Reprinted 1969 by
AUGUSTUS M. KELLEY · PUBLISHERS
NEW YORK NEW YORK 10010

LIBRARY OF CONGRESS CATALOGUE CARD NUMBER
66-21689

PRINTED IN THE UNITED STATES OF AMERICA
by SENTRY PRESS, NEW YORK, N. Y. 10019

PREFACE.

IN INTRODUCING a study upon a subject which has been so much written about as Adam Smith's ethical and economic theories, it is impossible of course to refer to all the useful and valuable books which I have consulted. The literature in the field is especially rich in works written during the latter half of the last century, under the influence of the German Historical School; but for the last twenty years the subject has received little attention, particularly in America. The two monographs of Hasbach—*Die allgemeinen philosophischen Grundlagen der von Francois Quesnay und Adam Smith begründeten politischen Oekonomie*, and *Untersuchungen über Adam Smith*—are of course of encyclopedic value, and I have consulted them freely. In general I have refrained from the use of footnotes except for the purpose of indicating the source of passages quoted, and the authority for statements possibly subject to question. To attempt to acknowledge my indebtedness by their use would be to burden the text unduly, even supposing the source of my indebtedness were always capable of statement.

What there is of original contribution—if that expression means much in a work of this kind—is to be found in the second and third chapters. The effect of the doctrine of natural law upon the development of English ethics is a subject which deserves a great deal more study than it has been possible to devote to it here, and to which I hope to return at some future time. What I have attempted to do is to show the significance of the contrast between this legalistic point of view and the ethical doctrine of sympathy as furnishing the background in which Adam Smith's economic theory developed, and in accordance with which both his economics and his ethics are to be interpreted. So far as I am aware the significance of the contrast between these two points of view has never been made clear by any previous student of Adam Smith's ethics and economics. But my purpose has been a broader one than simply to set forth this particular thesis; as the title indicates, it has been to study Adam Smith's moral philosophy in its relation to the various and often conflicting currents of eighteenth-century thought. Part of the matter of Chapters I and II has already appeared, with additions, in an article in the *Philosophical Review* of January of this year.

I take this opportunity of expressing my indebtedness and gratitude to Professor J. E. Creighton, of the Sage School of Philosophy, who not only suggested this subject, but has also assisted me very materially with criticisms and suggestions, both during the progress of my study and in the preparation of the manuscript for publication. My thanks are also due to Professor Ernest Albee for suggestions regarding the earlier chapters, and to all the members of the Sage School for inspiration and encouragement.

G. R. M.

Ithaca, N. Y., April 1923.

CONTENTS

PAGE

Introduction 1

CHAPTER

I. Eighteenth-Century Rationalism and Opposing Tendencies 12

II. The Doctrine of Sympathy 28

III. Justice Versus Benevolence 45

IV. The Economic Order 59

V. Conclusion 83

THE
ETHICAL AND ECONOMIC THEORIES OF ADAM SMITH

INTRODUCTION.

DURING the latter half of the eighteenth century, Scotland was the scene of a brilliant intellectual revival. The emphasis of the Scottish Kirk upon education had developed an appreciation for learning and a level of intelligence among the mass of the people in Scotland which was not then paralleled in any other country of Europe. At the head of the educational system stood the universities of Glasgow and Edinburgh, manifesting an intellectual vigor and a spirit of liberal inquiry which contrasted strikingly with the sluggishness and intolerance at Oxford and Cambridge. Edinburgh especially was the center of a brilliant group of thinkers. Matthew Bramble, in Smollett's *Humphrey Clinker*, writes under date of August 8 (1771): "Edinburgh is a hotbed of genius. I have had the good fortune to be made acquainted with many authors of the first distinction; such as the two Humes, Robertson, Smith, Wallace, Blair, Ferguson, Wilkie, etc., and I have found them all as agreeable in conversation as they are instructive and entertaining in their writings." He might have continued the enumeration with the names of Millar, Black, Hutton, Monboddo, Sir John Dalrymple, Dugald Stewart, and many others who contributed to make that city the most vigorous intellectual center of the British Isles. Moreover, the strong political sympathies which existed during the century between Scotland and France resulted in bringing this vigorous thought of the north into contact with the philosophical tradition of the Continent, and in particular with the varied interests of the French Enlightenment. It is enough to recall Hume's philosophy and the answer to his sceptical conclusions furnished by Reid and the other members of the 'common sense' school, to realize that the Scottish thought of the latter half of the eighteenth century is second in importance only to the critical philosophy of Kant.

With the possible exception of Hume, no one of this brilliant group has had greater influence upon subsequent thought than Adam Smith. The external circumstances of his life include nothing very striking or eventful. Born at Kirkcaldy in 1723, he went to Glasgow at the age of fourteen and remained a student at the University until 1740. There he came under the influence of Francis Hutcheson, Professor of Moral Philosophy, and the leader of the new spirit of liberal inquiry which was becoming characteristic of the Scottish universities. Hutcheson it was who first interested Adam Smith in the reading of Hume's *Treatise of Human Nature*, which appeared in 1739 and 1740, and which, as Smith found later, was under the ban at Oxford. Adam Smith's parents had apparently destined him for the church, and after his three years at Glasgow he went down to Oxford as an exhibitioner on the Snell Foundation. There he remained six years, the most of which he probably spent in private reading and study, since he tells us that at that time by far the greater part of the professors at Oxford had given up the pretense of lecturing. His public career began upon his return to his mother's home at Kirkcaldy, by his being invited to deliver a series of lectures on rhetoric and *belles-lettres* at Edinburgh. The lectures proved so successful that they were repeated the following year, and in 1749 he was called to Glasgow to occupy the chair of Logic, and afterwards that of Moral Philosophy, the same professorship which Hutcheson had held. The appointment was important for the development of Adam Smith's thought. We know from the accounts given by his students that he followed in his lectures the usual fourfold division of Moral Philosophy into Natural Theology, Ethics, Jurisprudence, and Political Economy; and the necessity of lecturing upon all these subjects was from the first a constant stimulus to the clarification and organization of his ideas.

In 1759 Adam Smith published the result of his ethical speculations in a book which bore the title, *The Theory of Moral Sentiments*. This work immediately aroused great interest, passed through six editions in the author's lifetime, and became as fashionable in the society at Paris, as Hume's works had been in the preceding decade. One result of the publication of the book was that it attracted the attention of Charles Townsend, the guardian of the young Duke of Buccleugh, who persuaded Smith to resign his professorship and accompany the young Duke as tutor and general companion on his travels in France. This connection lasted three years, and is outwardly the most eventful period in Smith's life. During this time the Scottish professor, whose fame had preceded him to Paris, came in personal touch with Continental thought, being cordially received by the foremost thinkers and public men of that ominous but brilliant period. After his return to Scotland he spent several years in scholarly retirement at Kirkcaldy, whence appeared in 1776 the *Inquiry into the Nature and Causes of the Wealth of Nations.* This book immediately made him world-famous, and he was offered a post as commissioner of customs at Glasgow in 1778. The remainder of his life was spent in performing the duties of this appointment, and in preparing new editions of the *Theory of Moral Sentiments* and the *Wealth of Nations.* He was also reported to be engaged on another work, the exact nature of which is not known, although it was probably the elaboration of his university lectures on jurisprudence. He died in 1790, however, before the work was completed, and the manuscript with others was destroyed by his own orders shortly before his death. The only papers saved were three essays on the history of the ancient sciences, and three on the nature of art; these were published by his executors in 1795 under the title *Essays on Philosophical Subjects.*

Between the two great works on which Adam Smith's fame rests there appears to be a very grave discrepancy. The moral and philosophical outlook of the *Wealth of Nations* seems at first sight to be utterly different from that of the *Moral Sentiments.* The ethical work is based upon the principle of sympathy, the capacity which the individual has of entering into the situation of another and bringing his own sentiments into accord with those of his fellow. In the economic work, however, the characteristic of the individual relied upon is the motive of self-interest. "It is not from the benevolence of the butcher, the brewer, or the baker, that we expect our dinner, but from their regard to their own interest. We address ourselves, not to their humanity but to their self-love, and never talk to them of our own necessities but of their advantages."[1] In the earlier work Adam Smith allies himself with Shaftesbury, Hutcheson and Butler in opposition to the egoistic ethical system of Hobbes; but in the later he shows the influence of one of the most radical of Hobbes's disciples, the notorious Dr. Mandeville. Moreover, in his ethical speculations Adam Smith evidently has in mind the vindication of certain spiritual values which the empiricist movement had cast doubt upon. At the same time in his other book, the *Wealth of Nations*, we seem to see an acceptance of the hedonism and materialism of the most extreme of the sensationalists. The apparent diversity in philosophical standpoint between these two works has given rise to a great deal of speculation, and among German scholars has even received a special designation, *Das Adam Smith Problem.*

The attempt has been made to find the explanation of this divergence in the external circumstances of Adam Smith's life. If we assume that there is a fundamental difference between the points of view of the two works, the explanation is close at hand that it was his residence in France during the years 1764–1766 which was responsible for his change of philosophical outlook. During his residence in France he frequently met Voltaire, Diderot, Condillac, Helvetius, d'Holbach, d'Alembert and other leaders of the Enlightenment. Moreover, we know that he was also a regular attendant at the meetings of the economic sect called the *Économistes*, which included Quesnay and his disciples in the Physiocratic movement. The economic doctrines of the *Wealth of Nations* show many points of resemblance to the doctrines which this sect maintained; and it is easy to suppose that Adam Smith's active interest in political economy began with his sojourn in Paris, and even that he borrowed his economic doctrines from the French economists. Fortunately it is easy now to demonstrate that the main principles of Adam Smith's own economic doctrines were formulated long before his journey to France. The subject of

[1] *Wealth of Nations*, I, 16.

Moral Philosophy as taught at Glasgow customarily included political economy, and we know from the account of Adam Smith's lectures given in Dugald Stewart's early memoir of his life that his lectures followed the usual plan. These lectures "comprehending the fundamental principles of his Inquiry [i.e. *Wealth of Nations*] were delivered at Glasgow as early as the year 1752 or 1753."[2] When we recall that the first of Quesnay's articles did not appear until 1756, we can see that the priority in time belongs to Adam Smith. Authoritative evidence as to the contents of these Glasgow lectures has recently been discovered in the form of a manuscript copy of the notes taken down by one of Adam Smith's students in 1763.[3] These notes correspond to the third and fourth parts of the lectures as described by Dugald Stewart. The possession of these lecture notes, representing the standpoint of Adam Smith in the year 1763, just before his journey to France, enables us to determine more accurately what contributions, if any, his contact with the French *Économistes* made to the economic doctrines of the *Wealth of Nations*. The specific points of difference between the economic part of the lectures and the later-published *Wealth of Nations* do not concern us here; the important point is that the same central conceptions are found in both works. The principle in the *Wealth of Nations* which seems to conflict with the ethical principle is the doctrine of self-interest; but the central importance of this moving principle of the economic order is recognized already in the *Lectures*, as is also its companion doctrine, the division of labor. It is accordingly evident that the inconsistency, if there be any, between Smith's ethical and economic thought is not to be explained as the result of a later change of interests. The hypothesis that Adam Smith's philosophical views underwent transformation as a result of French influences must be abandoned. The problem is not to reconcile the economic doctrines of 1776 with the ethical doctrines of 1759, but to reconcile the

[2] Stewart, *Works*, VII, 62.

[3] They consist of a manuscript copy made in 1766 from the original notes taken down by a student in 1763. They were first identified and published by Edwin Cannan in 1896, under the title *Lectures on Justice, Police, Revenue and Arms*.

economic and ethical doctrines taught at the same period, the period of his professorship at Glasgow.

Since, therefore, Smith cannot be regarded as having altered his point of view in later life, the problem is to understand the intellectual background and assumptions common to both the ethical and the economic doctrines. A great mass of literature has grown up in the attempt to establish a basis of unity between the two works. The attempt has been made by Delatour and Bagehot to find the unity in Adam Smith's purpose of writing a history of civilization, of which these two works formed a part.[4] Oncken has compared Smith with Kant, and found in his philosophy a dualism between the sensible *Güterwelt,* where men are mechanically moved by physical desires, and the *ethische Welt* of freedom.[5] Paszkowski in his monograph on Smith calls the *Wealth of Nations* a purely technological inquiry, concerned with man as he is, while the *Moral Sentiments* deals with man as he should be.[6] Lange reduces the benevolent impulses in the *Moral Sentiments* to reflected selfishness,[7] while Stephen and Jodl seem to agree in regarding the selfish impulses as the animating, the unselfish as the regulating principles in human nature.[8] The best known suggestion toward a solution of the difficulty is that of Buckle. He assumes that each work is a deductive inquiry based upon a certain set of premises, the *Moral Sentiments* based on the sympathetic, the *Wealth of Nations* on the selfish aspects of human nature; and that the two deductive processes taken together form a complete picture of human nature.[9]

None of these attempts at unification seem to me entirely satisfactory, while some of them, I think, show a misunderstanding of Adam Smith's purpose and method. It may be admitted, however, that each brings out a certain aspect of

[4] Delatour, *Adam Smith, sa vie, ses travaux, ses doctrines*, pp. 73-78; Bagehot, "Adam Smith as a Person," in *Works*, III, 269 ff.

[5] *Adam Smith und Immanuel Kant, passim.*

[6] *Adam Smith als Moralphilosoph*, p. 40.

[7] *History of Materialism*, III, 234 *n.*

[8] Stephen, *History of English Thought in the Eighteenth Century*, II, 321-322; Jodl, *Geschichte der Ethik*, I, 379-380.

[9] *History of Civilization in England*, II, 433-434.

the relation of his ethical and economic thought. The theory of Delatour and Bagehot emphasizes the fact that the *Moral Sentiments* and the *Wealth of Nations* are not to be taken as isolated or independent works, though the mere fact that Smith may have thought of them as two parts of a history of civilization would furnish only an external unity. It is difficult to see how Oncken's theory helps directly in interpreting Adam Smith, though it is pregnant with suggestions. Paszkowski is clearly mistaken when he calls the *Moral Sentiments* a study of man as he should be, while the *Wealth of Nations* is a study of man as he is; there are normative, as well as descriptive and empirical elements in both books.[10] To describe the benevolent impulses as essentially selfish, as Lange does, is to beg the question; and it is a complete misinterpretation to regard Smith as confining virtue to benevolence, or to understand his principle of sympathy as merely an altruistic impulse alongside the psychological impulse of self-love. Last of all, Buckle not only errs on most of the above points, but totally misconceives Smith's method, which is not purely inductive, as he asserts, but a combination of induction and deduction, as was common among the group of Scottish writers to which Adam Smith belonged.

Moreover, the difficulty, as it has presented itself to many of these writers, is largely factitious. To conceive of the "Adam Smith problem" as one of finding a formal reconciliation between the ethics and the *Wealth of Nations* is to set up a purely imaginary difficulty.[11] The crux of the question is the

[10] These criticisms, which are here necessarily stated in summary fashion, are later justified, either explicitly or implicitly, by the arguments of the following chapters.

[11] That there was no perception of such a difficulty in the minds of Adam Smith's contemporaries is evident from the memoir of Dugald Stewart above referred to. Stewart prefaces his discussion of the *Wealth of Nations* with a few remarks to illustrate "a connection between his system of commercial politics and those speculations of his earlier years in which he aimed more professedly at the advancement of human improvement and happiness" (*op. cit.*, VII, 52-56); and though he suggests several related problems which were at that time in the minds of thinking men—the relation of national wealth to morality, the human value of a profit and loss science, the contrast between modern economic policies and the wealth-discouraging policies of ancient states—yet there

place of self-interest in human excellence. Adam Smith accepts it as the primary factor in the economic situation. What is its position in the ethical theory? If we should find self-interest repudiated and benevolence substituted as the sole constituent of morality, we would be justified in bringing the charge of inconsistency. But this is not the case. On the contrary, Adam Smith parts company with the system of Hutcheson and refuses to define virtue solely in terms of benevolence. The frequent misunderstanding on this point is due to a superficial reading of the doctrine of sympathy in the *Moral Sentiments*. A discussion of the import of this doctrine, as a part of the philosophy of Adam Smith, will be given in a later chapter. It is sufficient here, in order to overthrow a very common misinterpretation of Smith, to point out that for him virtue is threefold, consisting of prudence, justice and benevolence. Prudence, or self-interest, the possession of which is to be regarded as an essential characteristic of a good man, is especially active and beneficial in the economic sphere, and is to be restrained only by the principle of justice. The activity of one individual in the pursuit of his own interest must not be allowed to hinder another in the same pursuit. Above the activity of self-interest restrained by justice there is a higher ethical principle, benevolence, which rules in the more intimate sphere of personal relationships. It is true that benevolence thus represents the fullest degree of human excellence; nevertheless it must be recognized that self-interest is not by any means peculiar to the economic work, but finds a definite and already recognized sphere of activity within the ethical theory as well. It is clear, therefore, that the charge that there exists a radical opposition between the ethical and the economic theories is thoroughly unjustified.[12]

Thus the problem found in connection with the work of Adam Smith is, at least as it is usually stated, an entirely

---

is no hint of the need for reconciling the view of human nature given in the *Wealth of Nations* with that given in the *Moral Sentiments*.

[12] *Moral Sentiments*, pt. vi. This has been most clearly set forth in the excellent monograph of Zeyss, *Adam Smith und der Eigennutz*, which should once for all dispose of *Das Adam Smith Problem*.

imaginary one. Smith did not receive his first impulse to the study of economics from his visit to France; he did not change from an idealist to a materialist during his later life. The characteristics of human nature employed in the *Wealth of Nations* are recognized in the *Moral Sentiments*; and the *Moral Sentiments* itself, in the last edition before his death [1790] contains an explicit statement, the more significant in view of the economic labors which had occupied his attention during the later years of his life, of the relation of the economic virtues to the whole of the moral life.

But the very unity discovered between the economic and the ethical theories inevitably raises a graver problem. This unity is based upon a distinction between the virtue of self-interest regulated by justice, and the virtue of benevolence —the first operative in the economic 'world,' and the other governing the sphere of personal relations. But what is the relation between these two fields of human activity? Looking at this question in the light of the later development of the classical economics it would seem that the ethical and the economic worlds are mutually exclusive. The economic doctrines that have developed since the early part of the nineteenth century under the influence of the *Wealth of Nations* portray an economic order governed by inexorable natural laws, such as the law of supply and demand, the law of diminishing returns, the law of population, the 'iron' law of wages, and the like. The elements in this economic order are 'economic men,' individuals actuated only by self-interest. On the other hand, these same individuals are also members of an order of personal relationships. What justification is there for treating them as governed solely by the economic motive? And if they are not governed by purely economic motives, whence comes the uniformity of the economic order, the necessity of the economic laws? If we admit the reality of the higher moral experience, the economic motive loses its universal application. Conversely, if we accept the laws of economics as universally valid, we cannot regard morality as anything but a fine illusion. It seems, therefore, that far from accepting the ethical and economic fields of activity as existing side by side, we must choose between them, or determine with more exactness than Adam Smith seems to have done the philosophical significance of the economic analysis and its relation to the concrete world of moral experience.

Although this is a problem which has concerned philosophy since the middle of the nineteenth century, yet it cannot be said that the philosophical and scientific value of the economic analysis has been clearly established. This failure has given rise to two contrary extremes of interpretation. On the one hand, scientific value has been denied to the economic analysis, both by exponents of the exact sciences and by moralists; by the former because they cannot find in its so-called laws the exactness which characterizes the laws of the more abstract sciences, and by the latter because they see in it a set of deductions never verified in concrete conditions. On the other hand, the acceptance of the economic laws as descriptive of the essential facts of social life, as expressing the real determining factors in history and civilization, has produced a variety of pseudo-philosophies based upon economic determinism, an economic interpretation of history, and the like. The consciousness of the need for properly placing the economic analysis with respect to these two extremes of interpretation has probably been the underlying reason why modern thinkers, in studying Adam Smith, have so easily found the traditional 'problem.'

The main value, therefore, of studying anew the relation of the ethical and economic theories of Adam Smith will consist in proceeding with this later problem explicitly in the foreground. While we cannot, without committing an anachronism, look for a direct apprehension of this problem in Adam Smith himself, nevertheless a study of the intellectual environment, so to speak, in which the classical economics had its origin and development cannot fail to prove suggestive as to the traditional presuppositions of economic science. In particular, an examination of Adam Smith's ethical theory will better enable us to understand the philosophical background of the *Wealth of Nations*. We shall begin the following study, therefore, by attempting a survey of the characteristic problems and methods of eighteenth-century thought, with a special reference to the ethical and economic theories which preceded Adam Smith's own works. A study of the implications of the two characteristic ethical principles developed in the *Moral Sentiments* will enable us to determine the contributions which that work made toward a social philosophy. Finally, the economic theory presented in the *Wealth of Nations* will be examined and compared with the social theory of the *Moral Sentiments* and with the characteristic concepts of eighteenth-century thought. The primary purpose of these chapters is, as above stated, to determine the philosophical background of the classical economics, and thereby make some contribution toward the problem of evaluating contemporary economic theory in so far as that science is still dominated by the classical tradition.

CHAPTER I.

Eighteenth-Century Rationalism and Opposing Tendencies.

THERE were two aspects of the philosophy of Locke which dominated the social philosophy of the eighteenth century in England and France, and conditioned almost all its speculation upon political and ethical questions. The first of these aspects was Locke's doctrine of individualism. The rigid form which this doctrine assumed in his thought was due to the influence of the rationalistic method, unconsciously employed by him in spite of his professed opposition to Cartesianism. In conformity with this analytic method, which sought the solution of a given problem by dividing it into ultimate elements clearly and distinctly conceived, Locke assumed that human individuals are the ultimate data of all human relations. Just as he attempted to separate the understanding into psychic elements and explain the whole by the parts, so he conceived of social phenomena in terms of isolated individuals, considered as the basic elements of which society is only a more complex derivative. From this individualism were derived the characteristic social and political problems of the century. The problem of greatest interest at that time was that of the nature of society, and the ground of the obligation to political obedience. Since society was considered as a union of independent individuals, political institutions had to be based upon some sort of an external tie, usually stated as a 'contract,' and regarded as explicit or tacit, historical or assumed, dissoluble or indissoluble, according to the temper of the thinker. The determination of the characteristics of the isolated individual —his motives to activity, his selfish or neutral or benevolent affections, and the like—became of supreme importance. The discussion which absorbed so much attention during the century as to whether or not society is 'natural' took place within the bounds of this individualism. Both those who asserted and those who denied the artificiality of social institutions based their appeal upon an analysis of the characteristics of the individual man. In general those moralists who found benevolent as well as selfish impulses in the individual were inclined to regard society as a natural union; while those who reduced all the activities of the individual to self-interest were obliged to regard the social union as imposing a restriction upon the freedom of individual activity, and therefore as contrary to nature. In both cases, however, the individual was the primary element by which the facts of the social unity were to be explained.

This preoccupation with the individual was characteristic of all the moralists and social philosophers of the first half of the century. The contract theories of Hobbes and Locke, though chronologically belonging to the preceding century, lived on and exercised a very active influence. Mandeville attempted to show that the material welfare of modern societies is based upon the active self-interest of the individual members.[1] The outcry which was occasioned in all quarters by the appearance of the *Fable of the Bees* was caused by the paradoxical form in which he stated his ethical theory, and not by the inadequacy of the individualistic premises from which he started. For the moralists who attempted to refute Hobbes and Mandeville were themselves conditioned by these same premises. Hutcheson, whose ethical theory asserts the priority of benevolence and thus is the very antithesis of the ethics of Hobbes, was unable to conceive of society as more than an aggregation of individuals externally united. Although he regarded benevolence as the principle which holds the social structure together, yet at the same time he held that society is based upon a contract, probably not historical, but at least tacit, between the component individuals for the purposes of greater prosperity and security.[2] Hume also attempted to derive society from independent and mutually antagonistic units. Man, he maintained, is unfit for society because of his

[1] *The Fable of the Bees; or Private Vices Public Benefits*, 1714.
[2] *System of Moral Philosophy*, 1755.

"limited generosity"—which seems to be only a euphemism for the wolfish qualities discovered by Hobbes. This limited generosity of man makes for natural hostility because of another factor, viz. the scarcity of economic goods, which are the objects of the self-interest of each individual. In order therefore to promote more efficiently their mutual interests by securing stability of property and adherence to agreements, men entered into a convention by which they agreed to abide by these principles of justice.[3]

Naturally the economic inquiries of the century involved the same individualistic assumptions. For the most part, the literature of the period which can be called economic consisted of short pamphlets on trade or taxes, or on some other material aspect of the public welfare, directed toward the solution of problems with which statesmen were especially concerned. Economics was still political economy and concerned itself with the study of the financial and material problems of political societies. These economic discussions seldom attempted an independent inquiry into the theoretical basis of society; they merely attempted to show how, on the basis of the social union established by the philosopher, the material welfare might be increased, either for the benefit of the individual or for the political advantage of the nation. Consequently the theoretical basis of the economic inquiries of the century was the same abstract individualism which we find in the general social philosophy. More than that, this individualistic philosophy seemed to possess a special fitness for explaining the economic aspects of society. It appeared most prominently in Mandeville, where the economic interest was supreme. Hutcheson was forced to abandon the principle of benevolence when he came to explain material progress. Benevolence is insufficient to inspire industrial progress, he admitted. "Self-love is really as necessary to the good of the whole as benevolence, as that attraction which causes the cohesion of the parts is as necessary to the regular state of the whole, as gravitation."[4] The result of this admission was a modification of the principle of universal

[3] *Treatise*, ed. Green and Grose, II, 258 ff.
[4] *Inquiry Concerning Moral Good*, Sec. vii, § viii.

benevolence by the recognition that benevolence varies in proportion to the nearness of relationship; but as Hume later showed, this is really a denial of the efficacy of universal benevolence. Hume himself, as we have seen, seemed to regard the social convention as motivated principally by economic interests. In short, when the economic aspects of the social order were brought into prominence, the conception of society as an external unity based upon mutual interest seemed more than ever the indispensable theoretical basis.

There was not wanting an occasional recognition of the inadequacy of this mechanical philosophy of society. Hume, who in so many other respects went beyond the limits of the thought of his century, not only abandoned the usually accepted contract theory, but expressed his dissatisfaction with his own theory of the social convention by distinguishing between the natural and the artificial virtues. The virtues which pertain to property, contract and right, and which are especially necessary in the economic life of society, he regarded as artificial, because founded upon a convention. They are upheld, indeed, by sympathy, but it is a sympathy with the welfare of society; and the order which they represent is an impersonal one. There are other virtues, such as courage, generosity, gratitude, which spring from the natural affections of men, and are approved and supported by personal sympathy.[5] This distinction of Hume's is essentially a limitation of the economic, contractual theory of society by the acknowledgment of another social order resting upon personal relations and extending to all the activities and values in human experience. We shall have occasion again in a later chapter to call attention to the logical importance of this distinction.[6]

Besides this individualistic method of formulating political and social problems, there was a second element in the philosophy of Locke which had far-reaching effects upon the thought of the eighteenth century. Logically regarded, this second element was a synthetic principle—the counterpart of the analytic method above sketched—by means of which the

[5] *Treatise, loc. cit.*, and II, 334 ff.

[6] *Infra*, p. 54.

various bits found by analysis are combined into one harmonious system. In Locke this principle of synthesis took on a religious coloring, as it did also in most of the thinkers of the eighteenth century. The adjustment of all the parts of the great machine to each other has been provided for by a great Designer: the synthesis of the parts discovered by analysis is found in the divine and rational plan. The characteristic feature of this principle of synthesis is its external character, its transcendency; it affirmed an abstract rational order of nature, of which the existing order was regarded as a more or less close approximation. The application to religion of this idea of an abstract rational order was the source of the deistic controversy which raged throughout the century: the deistic thinkers conceived of an absolute rational religion from which the positive historical faiths were greater or lesser departures. In like manner, this theory of a natural order was applied to positive law. Uniting itself with the Roman *jus gentium* and *jus naturale*, which had been revived in the preceding century, it posited an order of eternal and immutable relations subsisting between individuals on the basis of their common rational and social nature. The intellectualist moralists appealed to this order of natural justice to supply concrete filling for their formal ethical principles. Jurists attempted to deduce positive law from natural law, or at least used the latter as a criterion of the former. Political thinkers found in natural law the eternally valid principles which underlie all political arrangements, and by which existing constitutions can be judged; while the revolutionary philosophers based their contentions for the rights of man upon an appeal to the same rational order of nature. In almost all the social and ethical thought of the eighteenth century the final ground of argument was the consideration of an abstract natural order, either regarded as the legislation of Deity, or as existing in its own right because of its inherent rationality.

The doctrine of a 'natural order' is especially important in the history of economics, because on it was founded the first thorough-going economic theory, the system of thought formulated by the French *Économistes*.[7] These thinkers were of course interested not only in what are to-day regarded as economic phenomena, but also in the general laws of political societies. Nevertheless, their practical interests were distinctly directed toward the material welfare of the social order. In accordance with the prevailing mode of thought they had a firm faith in an unrealized natural order, based not upon history but upon abstract logic, which is *l'ordre naturel et essentiel des sociétés politiques*.[8] They appealed to history, or professed to, in order to show that in all societies there was a period in which the natural order prevailed, and that the actual order of most modern societies has diverged from that former condition. The natural order is therefore not the order which is actually found in operation, but the order which enlightened inquiry discovers to be the rational and most beneficent order. In the detailed carrying out of this conception of the natural order the Physiocrats showed themselves true representatives of the deistic philosophy. The natural order is the constitution which God himself has given to the universe. The social order has its own natural laws of divine origin, which if allowed unrestricted operation, will produce a perfect harmony between the interests of the individual and those of society. Since there exists this divinely established harmony between the individual and society, it follows that by pursuing his own interests the individual most happily furthers the welfare of the social body. The Physiocrats therefore placed a high value upon liberty; but since their practical interests were mainly economic, it is economic—and not political—liberty with which they are

[7] The founder and leader of the sect was Quesnay, court physician to Louis XV, whose first economic writing appeared in 1756. Other members of the sect were Dupont de Nemours, Mercier de la Rivière, Vincent de Gournay, the Abbé Baudeau. Turgot, though influenced by their doctrines, differed in some important respects. The name *Physiocratie* was first applied to their tenets by Dupont de Nemours in 1768, but the term *Physiocrates* apparently did not supplant the older appellation of *Économistes* until the middle of the last century. Cf. Coquelin, *Dictionnaire de l'Économie Politique*, art. "Physiocrates."

[8] The title of a work by Mercier de la Rivière, published in 1767, and on the whole the best exposition of Physiocratic doctrine. (In Daire, *Collection d'Économistes*, II, 445-642.)

concerned, the liberty of an individual to pursue his own material interests in the most advantageous way. They recognized, as Hume had done, that this kind of liberty is possible only in society, for only in coöperation with his fellow-men can the individual pursue his material welfare most advantageously. Hence they held no brief against society, or against the established political order as did Rousseau. Liberty meant for them freedom from the restrictions of government, and its antithesis was a misguided economic policy of the state. Their practical efforts were directed towards the removal of state intervention in spheres of activity which can be left to take care of themselves; so that in their conception of the relation of government to the economic life of the nation, as well as in the watchword—*laisser faire*—which expressed this conception, they can be regarded as the forerunners of nineteenth-century liberalism.

Although in the main the Physiocrats looked upon the natural order as an abstract ideal order of economic liberty, yet their conception of natural law was not exclusively a normative or ideal conception. Indeed its major importance for the history of social philosophy lies in the fact that it tended to become a scientific and positive method. For deistic thinkers in general the transition was easy from the legal to the scientific conception of natural law. The natural laws governing societies are the legislation of the divine lawgiver, hence are to a certain extent actually operative in existing societies. They are an expression both of the ideal order which reason would impose, and of the actual order of positive facts. This transition from the one conception to the other is clearly evident in the Physiocrats. The belief that political societies are subject to general laws analogous to the laws which govern the physical world was so important an element of their thought that one of their number rightly regarded it as furnishing the basis for a new science.[9] Many quotations could be given from their works to show the way in which they employed this fruitful point of view. One of its most striking results was the celebrated

[9] Dupont de Nemours, *Origine et progrès d'une science nouvelle.* (In Daire, *op. cit.*, II, 335-366.)

Tableau économique of Quesnay, published in 1758 and pronounced by Mirabeau one of the three great inventions of the human spirit. The *Tableau* was a graphic attempt to trace the circulation of wealth in human societies as a physician would trace the circulation of blood in the human body. Although the actual process of the circulation of wealth is now known to differ greatly from the course traced in Quesnay's diagram, yet it represented the first attempt to employ an organic concept in a scientific examination of the social order.[10] In a more general sense, the great importance of the Physiocrats in the history of social philosophy is that, along with such writers as Hume, Montesquieu and Adam Smith, they anticipated the sociological method, and perceived that social facts are capable of objective scientific treatment. It was on the basis of this objective examination of social facts that their characteristic economic doctrines were founded—the doctrine of the *produit net*, of the *impôt unique*, etc.—but while these doctrines were almost immediately refuted by Adam Smith, the method which gave rise to them was not only employed by him, but has been developed with increasing fruitfulness since their day.

On the whole, however, the ideal rather than the positive element predominated in Physiocratic thought. Their fundamental conception was that of a natural social order; and this natural order was the economic régime which enlightened eighteenth-century thinkers would have liked to see established—a régime based upon individual initiative and *laisser faire*. As such it incorporated a rational ideal; and though many elements of this ideal were borrowed from observation of the actual facts of social life, yet these facts were detached from their concrete setting and subjected to an arbitrary synthesis. Moreover, the ideal economic régime of the Physiocrats partook of the defects of all the eighteenth-century pictures of the natural order. The harmony which it expressed was of an external sort, imposed from without upon the constituent elements, not produced from within by the mutual adjustments of the parts to one another. Instead of an organic unity pro-

[10] Cf. Gide et Rist, *Histoire des doctrines économiques*, 4th ed., p. 10.

duced by the processes of growth and adaptation, it posited a mechanical unity eternally given.

Like the abstract individualism of the century, this conception of a timeless natural order, though expressive of the prevailing habits of thought, was already being criticized as an inadequate philosophy of society. The natural order, under all the forms it assumed, was necessarily thought of as an absolute order, divorced from all historical conditions. But the historical spirit was asserting itself even in the eighteenth century, and was introducing the idea of the relativity of all social institutions to the historical conditions in which they arise. Montesquieu's *Esprit des lois*, which appeared in 1748, directly opposed the rationalistic method of the century by applying the historical method to the study of laws and social institutions. Like the *Economistes* Montesquieu regarded social phenomena as subject to laws, but not to the laws of an absolute rational order. Political and social institutions are relative to the needs which they serve, to the spirit of the people among whom they exist, to climatic conditions, and above all, to the other political and social institutions with which they coexist. Even before the appearance of the work of Montesquieu, Hume also had made valuable contributions to the development of the historical method. In his criticism and rejection of the theory of an actual historical contract forming the basis of political obligation, in his disproof of the deistic belief in a primal revelation of the rational religion (for which he substituted a theory of the development of monotheism from an originally polytheistic religion), and above all in his conception of the national groups as possessing a solidarity of life and an individuality of their own, Hume did much to undermine the faith in the older rationalistic method and prepare the way for the historical point of view.[11] Moreover, the whole group of thinkers to which Hume belonged, influenced both by contact with France and the work of Montesquieu, and by the very tradition of the Scottish universities, which had long made Pufendorf and Grotius objects of study, developed the induc-

[11] Cf. Sabine, Geo. H., "Hume's Contribution to the Historical Method," in *Philosophical Review*, XV, 17-38.

tive historical method with great energy. The *Wealth of Nations*, as we shall see in a later chapter, contains much that is historical in character; and it is well known that Adam Smith's projected work on jurisprudence was to have followed the lines of investigation laid down by Montesquieu.[12] This method of studying social institutions ran counter to the established modes of thought, and was found as yet only in isolated instances; yet it is clear that the unhistorical and rationalistic philosophy did not hold undisputed possession of the field.

Meanwhile the rationalism of the century was being attacked from another and more immediately vulnerable side. From the very beginning of the century the school of British and Scottish moralists known as the 'sentimentalists' had maintained that the abstract reason cannot furnish the basis of the moral experience; that this basis must be found in the feelings, or the sentiments, or in a moral sense. The consequence of the development of this anti-rationalistic point of view in ethics was to call into question not only rationalism in ethics, but also the general rationalistic method of which rationalist ethics was only one application.

Two of the principal elements in this rationalistic method were, as we have seen, its appeal to an abstract rational order, and its radical individualism. Of these two elements the sentimentalists rejected from the very beginning the appeal to an abstract rational order. The contrast between their position and that of their opponents, the intellectualists, is instructive in this connection. The intellectualists were impressed with the universality and the obligatoriness of the moral law; they therefore affirmed that the moral law is rational, i.e. based upon certain eternal and immutable relations of things; and that the morality of a particular act is derived from its conformity to these eternal relations. The difficulty in this

[12] Buckle strangely neglects this movement when he characterizes the Scottish thought of the century as entirely deductive (*Hist. of Civilization in Eng.*, II, 410 ff.). It is possible to mention such Scottish writers as Kames, Millar, Dalrymple, Ferguson, Gilbert Stuart, as well as Adam Smith himself, who not only professed their indebtedness to Montesquieu, but also published works of a distinctly historical character.

position was that in insisting upon universality the intellectualists often secured only the empty formalism of mathematical or identical propositions; while to take refuge in the principle of utility to provide content was in a sense desertin the cause they undertook to defend. Moreover, the conception of reason as mere ratiocination, or as the perception of general rules, made it an inactive principle; and against this it was easy to show, as Hume did, that reason can never give rise to conscience. The perception of these difficulties led the sentimentalists to deny that reason divorced from feeling is the basis of the moral judgment. Instead of the universality and obligatoriness of the moral law, they emphasized the unreflective and spontaneous character of approbation and its reference not to general rules but to particular concrete acts. Above all, the moral law prompts to action, and thus must be based upon the active part of human nature, the sentiments or passions. While this position relieved them of some of the difficulties of their opponents, yet it eventually involved the sentimentalists themselves in a more difficult problem, viz. the problem of explaining the universality and obligatoriness of the moral law. If the moral judgment is based merely upon the feelings, how can it be more than a personal judgment? If reason is rejected, how is an objective moral judgment possible?

The individualism of the rationalistic method was at first accepted without question by the sentimentalists; only in process of time did they come to realize that in order to refute the ethical scepticism of Hobbes and Mandeville it was necessary to advance beyond the unreflective individualism which had given rise to it. The egoistic ethics—the logical consequence of conceiving the individual as a complete and self-contained unit—was manifestly inconsistent with the plain facts of the moral experience; but instead of attacking the fallacious conception of individuality, the moralists at first attempted to base a refutation of egoism upon the same individualistic assumption. They attempted to show that the analysis of the individual consciousness had been incomplete, that there are 'other-regarding' as well as 'self-regarding' impulses in the individual. But the impossibility of logically maintaining the existence of other-regarding impulses and at the same time holding to the assumption of rigid individualism led them gradually but surely to a consciousness of the real difficulty. Instead of an absolute element, the individual came to be interpreted more and more in the light of the social relations which he maintains. The facts of individuality were gradually seen to be relative to social facts and dependent upon explanatory principles that transcend the individual. This transition from an abstract to a more adequate conception of individuality can be clearly traced in the sentimental moralists of the eighteenth century.

Neither Shaftesbury nor Hutcheson made any real advance over the radical individualism of Hobbes. It is true that Shaftesbury was influenced by the ethical tradition of antiquity as well as by the new individualism, and thus was free from some of the extreme statements of the latter found in Hobbes and Mandeville. Instead of the individual as a self-sufficing unit, he set up the species as the ultimate goal of all individual activities.[13] Hence he found within the individual other affections besides purely selfish ones; man is led also by social affections, by an appreciation of his own position as a part of a systematic whole whose good he should promote. Virtue therefore consists in the proper harmony of the private and social affections. But in spite of his pretensions, Shaftesbury never really got beyond the individualistic point of view. The social affections found in the individual were just so many more characteristics, accepted as given, individual endowments provided by the author of nature who designed the harmony of the universe. The principle of synthesis was still external, and Shaftesbury's position reduced itself to the contention that Hobbes's analysis of the individual had been incomplete. He made occasional suggestions as to the self-refuting character of individualism, but failed to develop them in a manner consistent with the remainder of his thought. Hutcheson, too, proceeded in much the same manner.[14] He maintained that man's interests are not wholly self-centered, that he has also a desire

[13] *Inquiry Concerning Virtue*, 1699; *Characteristics*, 1711.
[14] *Inquiry Concerning Moral Good and Evil*, 1725.

for the good of the whole of humanity. Shaftesbury had found virtue in propriety, or the proper harmony of the selfish and benevolent affections; but Hutcheson developed Shaftesbury's principle of love for the species and asserted that benevolence constitutes the primary object of moral approbation. This benevolence is like the principle of gravitation in the physical world; it extends to all bodies in the universe, but varies inversely with the distance. The moral universe would thus be for Hutcheson a system of externally related units of the same logical character as the physical world revealed by scientific analysis.

A more fruitful line of thought was opened up by Hutcheson when he attempted to distinguish between natural good and moral good. The moral judgment must be distinguished from judgments of pleasure or pain, for the characteristic quality of the moral judgment is its disinterestedness. The perception of advantage or disadvantage can never reverse the moral judgment, hence is something distinct from it. Natural good is that quality in an object or an action which brings pleasure to our sense-perception; moral goodness secures the love or approval of disinterested spectators. Natural good is therefore individual, and is the object of interest and self-love, but moral good is desired because of love for the welfare of mankind. Thus Hutcheson clearly recognized that the essential elements in the moral experience transcend the individual; but when he attempted to show how this is possible he exposed the limitations of his assumptions. By taking up Shaftesbury's vague concept of the 'moral sense' and making it the basis of the moral judgment, Hutcheson really deserted the distinction between natural and moral good. If the moral sense is on the same plane as the other natural senses, of sight, hearing, etc. (a thing which Hutcheson stoutly maintained in spite of its scientific absurdity), then, after all, the sanction of morality is no different in kind from the sanction of natural good.[15] What Hutcheson was aiming at was to establish the disinterested

[15] *On the Nature and Conduct of the Passions and Affections,* Sec. i, §i; *Illustrations upon the Moral sense,* Sec. i. Cf. Adam Smith's criticism of this theory in *Moral Sentiments,* pt. vii, sec. iii, ch. 3.

character of the moral experience as distinguished from the individual character of pleasure and pain; but the moral sense theory utterly fails to justify any such distinction. We are back again at the individual and his individual pleasures and pains, from which it seems there can be no appeal.

The most important modification of the individualistic premises was made by Hume. His contribution to the theory of knowledge was purely negative—a denial of causal relations in the outer world of experience, a denial of real unity in the personal consciousness. But when discussing the question of morals he was not content to remain at the sceptical position which his own assumptions would necessitate, and introduced an over-individual factor to account for the moral experience. He accepted without question the objectivity of the moral judgment, and saw that in this possession of objectivity it differs from an individual judgment of self-love. When a man makes a moral judgment he must "depart from his private and particular situation, and must choose a point of view common to him with others; he must move some universal principle of the human frame, and touch a string to which all mankind have an accord and symphony."[16] The basis of such an objective judgment can be found, not in self-love, but in some over-individual principle which makes all mankind one. This over-individual factor is variously called—in the *Enquiry* —sympathy, or benevolence, or humanity; its psychological explanation is given in the *Treatise*, where it is uniformly called sympathy. If each individual is subject only to his own pleasure and pain, how can he approve an act which affords pleasure to another, or an act which is useful to the whole of society? Such experience is possible because the consciousnesses of individuals are not mutually isolated. The idea of another man's pleasure or pain, by long or frequent association with my own consciousness, becomes converted into an impression of my own pleasure or pain.[17] Thus it is evident that sympathy meant for Hume the actual participation of one individual in the sentiments of another; it is the "principle of communica-

[16] *Essays*, II, 248.
[17] *Treatise*, II, 110 ff.

tion" by which the individuals of a social group are made into a unity; it is "that propensity we have to sympathize with others, and to receive by communication their inclinations and sentiments, however different from, or even contrary to our own."[18] He develops this idea in many other passages of the *Treatise*. "The bare opinion of another, especially when enforced with passion, will cause an idea of good or evil to have an influence upon us, which would otherwise have been entirely neglected. This proceeds from the principle of sympathy or communication."[19]

Hume's adoption of the "principle of sympathy or communication" as the basis of the moral experience is one of the most significant facts in eighteenth-century ethics, because as used by him it really amounted to an abandonment of the individualistic way of stating the ethical problem. It implicitly denied that the characteristics of the individual are given, and that the explanation of the moral experience is to be found by an analysis of these given characteristics. It implied that, on the contrary, the true explanation of the moral experience is to be found in the association of individuals with one another; i.e. that we must recognize the social as well as the individual factor in the development of the moral consciousness. This point becomes clear if we contrast Hume's doctrine of sympathy with that of Hutcheson or Shaftesbury. In these writers sympathy was assumed as a characteristic of human nature, as a synonym for compassion, or pity, and as one of the unselfish impulses. But this unselfish impulse was considered as given, along with the other characteristics of human nature, and involved no abandonment of the abstract individualism. Hutcheson had considered the possibility of basing morality upon sympathy, but rejected it; for him benevolence must be already assumed in order to account for sympathy. When Hume, however, referred to sympathy as "the principle of communication," and as "the source of all moral distinctions," it is clear that he had in mind something entirely different from what Hutcheson meant by the

[18] *Op. cit.*, II, 111.
[19] *Ibid.*, II, 205.

same word. Sympathy, for Hume, was not the object of approbation, but the necessary psychological and metaphysical basis of all moral judgments, whether of approbation or of disapprobation. The objectivity of the moral judgment is possible because the individual participates, through sympathy, in the sentiments of others; his feelings are not merely the products of his own individual consciousness, but have been developed in the presence of the sentiments of his fellow-men. In this way the moral judgment, though preserving its basis in the feelings and thus remaining in intimate contact with the concrete data of experience, becomes objective by being founded on an over-individual principle.[20]

Thus the moralists of the sentimental tradition were forced beyond the narrow individualism with which they began. It gradually came to be seen that the ethical problem was insoluble when proposed in terms of externally related individuals; if the true character of the moral experience is to be explained, the individual must not be taken in isolation, but regarded as himself the expression of social factors. As the representatives of the sentimental school had from the start discarded the appeal to abstract reason, it is clear that the general tendency of their thought was to discredit the rationalistic method of the century, not only in its application to ethics, but also when concerned with social and political problems. This school therefore maintained a current of thought in more or less latent opposition to the prevailing social and political rationalism of the latter half of the century.

This is the ethical tradition of which Adam Smith's moral theory is the continuation. A pupil of Hutcheson, a life-long friend and admirer of Hume, Adam Smith was at the beginning and remained throughout his life in close sympathy with the point of view and methods of the sentimental school. We have attempted to make clear the characteristics of this school, and their relation to the more general characteristics and presuppositions of eighteenth-century thought. It remains now to examine Adam Smith's ethics on its own account.

[20] For a fuller discussion of Hume's use of the principle of sympathy, cf. the author's article, "The Significance of the Doctrine of Sympathy in Hume and Adam Smith," *Philosophical Review*, XXXII, 60-78.

CHAPTER II.

The Doctrine of Sympathy.

IN ATTEMPTING a critical interpretation of the *Theory of Moral Sentiments* it may be well to approach the analysis of the moral experience under the schema which Adam Smith himself has constructed. Smith was the first English moralist to distinguish clearly between the problem of the content of morality and the problem of the nature of the moral faculty. A lengthy section of the *Moral Sentiments* is devoted to an analysis and criticism of preceding ethical theories in the light of these two problems; and this section is valuable not only as one of the first sketches of the history of ethics, but also as affording us an immediate understanding of Adam Smith's own point of departure. With regard to the nature of morality, he distinguished three different historical theories: first, the classical doctrine that virtue consists in propriety, revived in modern times by Shaftesbury and the intellectualists; second, the theory which asserts that virtue is merely utility or prudence, as maintained by the Epicureans; and third, the theory which identifies virtue with benevolence, held by the ancient Eclectics, Neo-Platonists, the Christian moralists, Cudworth, More, Hutcheson, and others. To the problem of the nature of the moral faculty, Smith recognized a like variety of answers. The moral judgment was founded on self-love by Hobbes, Pufendorf and Mandeville; on reason, by Cudworth and the intellectualists; on a special sense called the moral sense, by Hutcheson; while still others found its basis in the moral sentiments in general, or sympathy.[1]

However interesting it would be to examine in detail Adam Smith's own answers to these two questions, we must confine ourselves to a brief consideration of the two characteristic doctrines of his system. These are: (1) the doctrine that the

[1] *Moral Sentiments*, pt. vii.

moral judgment is based upon sympathy; and (2) the dualism of virtues, or the contrast between justice and benevolence. Both of these aspects of his theory have been referred to in the preceding pages, but since they are especially important for our understanding of the relation of his ethical theory to his economics we shall examine them more closely with the purpose of determining their wider implications.

Many misinterpretations of Adam Smith's ethics have proceeded from a too facile reading of the doctrine of sympathy. We have discussed in the preceding chapter Hume's use of the principle of sympathy as the basis of the moral judgment, and we have seen that it implied the adoption of an over-individual principle. Sympathy was for Hume (in the *Treatise*, at least) not another psychological trait existing in the individual alongside of the passion of self-love, but it was the capacity of participating in the sentiments of others, whereby the moral judgment becomes objective. Adam Smith used sympathy in essentially the same way as Hume did in the *Treatise*. It was the principle of communication by means of which the sentiments of one individual influence and are influenced by the sentiments of his fellow-men. It would be as erroneous, therefore, in Adam Smith's case as it would be in Hume's to regard this use of sympathy as merely a further application of Hutcheson's doctrine of benevolence. To say that Smith's ethics is based upon sympathy does not mean that sympathy is the content of morality, but means rather that sympathy is the principle of communication between individuals which makes possible the moral judgment. This point will become clear if we sketch the doctrine of the sympathetic basis of the moral experience as it is developed in the *Moral Sentiments*.

The fundamental principle in Adam Smith's ethical theory is that all moral judgments are based upon an imaginary change of situation, whereby the individual judging places himself in the situation of the individual judged, and feels to some extent as his own the sentiments and passions of the latter. This participation in the feelings of others is sympathy. "However selfish soever man may be supposed, there are evidently some principles in his nature, which interest him in the fortune of others, and render their happiness necessary to him."[2] The misery and misfortune of others excite a similar passion in the spectator; and likewise he takes pleasure in beholding their happiness. This identification, as it were, of ourselves with others is instinctive. When we see a stroke aimed at the leg or arm of another we immediately draw back our own, as if it were threatened. In watching a rope-walker we ourselves feel a sense of relief when he reaches the platform at the end of his rope. The moral judgment is only the development of this primitive form of imaginary identification of ourselves with others. Briefly stated, when we pass judgment upon another we merely perceive an agreement or disagreement of his passions with what our own would be if in his situation. There is a pleasure in an accord of sentiments; and if after the imaginary change of situation has taken place we perceive that his emotions are such as would accord with our own in his situation, we approve and call them good; and in the contrary case, when we perceive that our own passions do not accord with his, we disapprove; and moral approbation is nothing but the perception of this accord, as disapprobation is nothing but the perception of this dissonance of sentiments.[3]

Adam Smith applies this principle of a sympathetic accord of sentiments to a great many varieties of circumstances in which judgments of moral worth take place. The main distinction which he introduces is that between judgments of propriety and impropriety, and judgments of merit and demerit. "In the suitableness or unsuitableness, in the proportion or disproportion which the affection seems to bear to the cause or object which excites it, consists the propriety or impropriety, the decency or ungracefulness of the consequent action. In the beneficial or hurtful nature of the effects which the affection aims at, or tends to produce, consists the merit or demerit of the action."[4] In refusing to confine morality to judgments of merit or demerit—i.e. to considerations of beneficial or injurious consequences—Adam Smith, like Shaftesbury, con-

[2] *Op. cit.*, pt. i, sec. i, ch. 1.
[3] *Ibid.*, pt. i, sec. i, chs. 1-3.
[4] *Ibid.*, pt. i, sec. i, ch. 3.

tinues the ethical tradition of antiquity, in opposition to the more common utilitarian attitude of his contemporaries. In both classes of judgments, however, the principle involved is the same—the sympathetic appreciation of the sentiments of the other individuals concerned, and a comparison of sentiments based upon this sympathetic appreciation.

Sympathy means, therefore, something more than pity or compassion; it signifies essentially a participation in the feelings of others, and it is only through the ability of passing beyond the limits of individuality that a moral judgment is possible. The full import of the principle of sympathy becomes manifest when Smith discusses the foundation of our judgments concerning our own sentiments and conduct. We approve or disapprove of ourselves by identifying ourselves in imagination with the spectators of our actions, and perceiving whether under such conditions we can or cannot sympathize with our own conduct. "We can never survey our own sentiments and motives, we can never form any judgment concerning them, unless we remove ourselves, as it were, from our own natural station, and endeavor to view them as at a certain distance from us. But we can do this in no other way than by endeavoring to view them with the eyes of other people, or as other people are likely to view them."[5] All our judgments of ourselves have a secret reference to the judgments of others. A human creature who should grow up in some solitary place, without any communication with his kind, would have no idea of virtue and vice. The moral sentiments are the result of living in society; we know ourselves to be virtuous or vicious, not from any inner source of moral insight, but from experience gained of the approbation and disapprobation of our fellow-men.

Certain outstanding phenomena in our personal experience seem at first sight to disprove this theory of the social origin of our moral judgments. In judging ourselves we demand not only that we be the recipients of the approval of our fellow-men, but also that we be worthy of receiving their approval, and the two demands are not the same. But Adam Smith does not here abandon the social principle; instead he

[5] *Op. cit.*, pt. iii, ch. 1.

clarifies it by introducing the important concept of the impartial spectator. The phenomena we have just mentioned indicate that we often appeal from the judgment of the actual spectators of our action to the judgment of future better informed spectators, or to what the judgment of the present spectators would be if they knew all the circumstances. We appeal to the sympathies of the impartial spectator, who is freed from the limitations of their knowledge and personal situation.[6]

Smith's rejection of utility as the foundation of morality is but a further expression of his belief that the moral experience is a social and not an individual affair. He does not deny that there is a beauty and a deformity which characters possess because of their usefulness or detriment to the individual or to society, but he maintains that the perception of such beauty is not all there is in the moral approbation. Nor is the perception of utility the immediate ground of our approbation of actions or sentiments. This approbation is based upon an appeal to the impartial spectator, not upon a perception of their utility. The real difficulty is that utility is an individual concept, and applies only to individual experience, whereas morality is social. A solitary individual could very well acquire ideas of the utility of his own actions and of the beauty of that utility, but without contact with society could never have applied to them the specific character of moral approbation.[7]

This is the substance of Adam Smith's analysis of the origins of the moral judgment. Strictly speaking, it does not in itself presuppose any concrete theory of the nature of morality. It has only been shown that, whatever may be the content of morality, the basis of moral approbation and disapprobation is found in the principle of sympathy. And this we have found to mean that the individual moral judgment becomes possible only because the individual participates in the moral judgments of other individuals with whom he in imagination identifies himself. We may say that the moral judgment of the individual is the expression of the social consciousness. It is evident that this is a new point of view in British ethics. We

[6] *Op. cit.*, pt. iii, ch. 2.
[7] *Ibid.*, pt. iv, ch. 2.

have already seen that the usual method used by eighteenth-century moralists was to construct the moral and social order as a derivative of the facts revealed in individual experience. The social order was recognized as having an influence upon the individual, it is true; but only to the extent of developing the moral consciousness already existing in him in embryo. Morality was supposed to find its ultimate basis of validity in some trait of the individual, either his selfishness or his altruism, his benevolence or his love for the species. The theory of Adam Smith openly abandons this individualistic method. The moral world is something independent of the individual thinker. His moral judgment is based, not upon an inner intuition of rational truth, nor upon a divine revelation, but upon the reflected sentiments of other individuals; and the moral sentiments of himself and those of his fellow-men, mutually supporting and influencing one another, produce the objective order of moral standards. At the same time this objective moral order is not a transcendent rational order, like the order of immutable truth to which the intellectualist moralists appealed, but an order immanent in human experience, and varying with the conditions of experience.

It is this (to the eighteenth century, paradoxical) conception of a whole which is more stable than any one of its component parts, that has been the source of nearly all the criticisms brought against the theory of Smith. We shall discuss briefly the most important of these criticisms in order to bring out more clearly the social implications of the doctrine of sympathy and its importance for the philosophy of society.

The most obvious criticism, from the point of view of rationalistic ethics, is that this system fails to provide for the universality and the necessity which are essential to the moral law. The moral judgment appeals to an invariable standard, it is said, and therefore cannot be founded upon such an unstable phenomenon as sympathy. Sympathy is too fleeting, too uncertain, too variable in intensity and range to serve as the moral criterion. This in substance has been the main criticism brought against Adam Smith's ethics from the time of Thomas

Brown to Leslie Stephen.[8] To what extent is this criticism justified?

No one has ever recognized more clearly than Adam Smith the danger that the moral judgment in particular instances may be warped by the subjective attitude of the individual concerned. "To the selfish and original passions of human nature, the loss or gain of a very small interest of our own, appears to be of vastly more importance, excites a much more passionate joy or sorrow, a much more ardent desire or aversion, than the greatest concern of another with whom we have no particular connection."[9] An earthquake which would swallow up all the inhabitants of China would cause less real disturbance to an ordinary man than the loss of his little finger. Nevertheless the virtuous man takes the universal point of view, he looks upon himself as others see him, and he recognizes that he would be the object of the disapprobation of all his fellow-men if he should act purely on the basis of his immediate interests and sympathies. But how is it possible to attain this universal point of view in the midst of passion? The effect of emotion, especially of strong self-love, is to render us insensible to the disapprobation of our fellow-men, so that we feel nothing but the impulse toward our own satisfaction. In such circumstances the only recourse is to appeal to certain general rules which we have formed from experience as to the propriety or impropriety of actions, and to act according to them as forming an immutable basis of morality. This is Adam Smith's doctrine of conscience. "Our continual observations upon the conduct of others, insensibly lead us to form to ourselves certain general rules concerning what is fit and proper either to be done or to be avoided. Some of their actions shock all our natural sentiments. We hear everybody about us express the like detestation against them. . . . We thus naturally lay down to ourselves a general rule that all such actions are to be avoided, as tending to render us odious, contemptible, or punishable, the objects of all those sentiments for which we have the

[8] Brown, *Lectures on the Philosophy of the Human Mind*, IV, 80-104; Stephen, *History of English Thought in the Eighteenth Century*, II, 74 ff.

[9] *Moral Sentiments*, pt. iii, ch. 3.

greatest dread and aversion. Other actions, on the contrary, call forth our approbation, and we hear everybody around us express the same favorable opinion concerning them. We . . . . thus naturally lay down to ourselves a rule of another kind, that every opportunity of acting in this manner is carefully to be sought after. It is thus that the general rules of morality are formed."[10] When these general rules have been established on the basis of the concurring sentiments of mankind, "we frequently appeal to them as to the standards of judgment. . . . They are upon these occasions commonly cited as the ultimate foundations of what is just and unjust in human conduct."[11] Thus when the individual is confronted with a situation where a moral choice is necessary he is not left to the fleeting and transient sentiments of himself or of his immediate fellow-men, but he finds a body of moral rules at hand for regulating his conduct. Moreover, the teachings of theology may reënforce the authority of his conscience by leading him to look upon these rules as laws of God. It is clear, therefore, that Adam Smith's system by no means leaves the individual to his own capricious sympathies; for any given individual the moral order is objectively real and necessary.

Evidently, however, these general rules will appear in a different light according as they are regarded as authoritative principles for the particular individual and the particular instance, or as having had an origin and development in experience. Adam Smith's purpose seems to be twofold: to show the moral sentiments as originating in social experience, and at the same time as authoritative rules for the guidance of the individual. Necessarily the close juxtaposition of the two conceptions leads to some ambiguity and confusion. If he had been writing a hundred years later he would have made his meaning clearer by explicitly introducing the idea of racial experience: the moral standards are developed in the experience of the race, but possess primary and authoritative status with respect to the individual. In spite of frequent ambiguity, however, it is clear that Smith has seized upon the important

[10] *Op. cit.*, pt. iii, ch. 4.
[11] *Loc. cit.*

fact that the moral order is immanent in social experience. Indeed if we follow somewhat further the implications of this doctrine of conscience we can see that it really prepares the way for a conception of moral progress in society. Conscience, it recognizes, is by no means an absolute standard. It is absolute for the vast majority of mankind, but there are certain individuals "of the happiest mould" who "are capable of suiting with exact justness, their sentiments and behavior to the smallest difference of situation," and can therefore dispense with regard for the general rules of conscience.[12] Since, as we have already seen, the general rules of conscience are themselves the result of the individual's contact with the social consciousness, it may not be too much to interpret this second and higher stage of moral experience as consisting in a greater sensitiveness to the social demands, toward which the lower stage of obedience to general rules only gradually approximates.[13]

An examination of the concept of the impartial spectator—an appeal to whose sympathies establishes the validity of both stages of the moral experience—will render more evident the social character of Adam Smith's theory of morals. The theory of the impartial spectator has been the subject of much criticism at the hands of Cousin, Jouffroy and Delatour. It was pronounced by Cousin the ruin of the system.[14] To introduce the abstract impartial spectator was, in the opinion of Jouffroy and Delatour, to abandon the principle that the moral judgment is based upon social experience.[15] For the impartial spectator, it is maintained, is a fiction of my own mind; hence in appealing to his judgment I in reality abandon the appeal to the sentiments of my fellow-men and find my authority in a fictitious personality, the representative of my own subjective standard. But this criticism seems to be based upon a too literal interpretation of the theory in question; in order to understand the impartial spectator, we must interpret it in

[12] *Op. cit.*, pt. iii, ch. 5.

[13] This point is further borne out by the contrast which Smith introduces between justice and benevolence. Cf. *infra*, pp. 54 ff.

[14] *Philosophie écossaise*, p. 180.

[15] Jouffroy, *Cours de droit naturel*, II, 1-54; Delatour, *Adam Smith*, pp. 90 ff.

accordance with the spirit of the system of which it forms a part. The chief significance of the theory of the impartial spectator is that—like the doctrine of conscience just discussed—it introduces a regulative principle into the moral order of individual sympathies. In passing judgment upon ourselves it is not possible to rely purely upon the accidental sympathies of the spectators by whom we are surrounded. If the system had no better basis it would be a thinly disguised egoistic ethics—a charge which Smith is careful to answer in advance. "Sympathy is by no means to be regarded as a selfish principle," he consistently maintains. Nor in our judgments of others are we subject only to the contingent conditions of our susceptibilities. We rightly recognize that there is a certain propriety in our sympathies, and that at times we must ignore their immediate manifestations and appeal to a more permanent authority. To this higher authority he has given the name of the impartial spectator.[16] The impartial spectator is the personification of that which is permanent, universal, rational, natural, in the phenomena of sympathy. Some sympathies are merely accidental and contingent; their contraries may with equal likelihood be present the next moment; in fact, all sympathies partake in a greater or less degree of this quality of contingency. But taken together in their mass, there is a stability about the phenomena of sympathy which is not found in the inspection of individual instances; and it is these permanent stable elements of sympathy which we regard as embodied in the personality of the impartial spectator.

If now we bear in mind that sympathy is for Smith, as for Hume, the principle which fits man for society, it becomes evident that the conception of the impartial spectator as the personification of the norms of sympathy is closely bound up with the welfare of the social order. Natural, or rational sympathy is that sympathy which best furthers the existence of men together in society; and as the embodiment of such sympathy, the impartial spectator is the guardian of the social welfare. The following passage is a clear indication that the impartial spectator is a social concept: "Nature, when she

[16] *Moral Sentiments*, pt. iii, ch. 2.

formed man for society, endowed him with an original desire to please and an original aversion to offend his brethren. . . . But this desire of the approbation, and this aversion to the disapprobation of his brethren would not alone have rendered him fit for that society for which he was made. Nature, accordingly, has endowed him not only with a desire of being approved of, but with a desire of being what ought to be approved of."[17] Remembering that this desire of praise-worthiness is the appeal to the impartial spectator, as distinguished from the love of praise, which is an appeal to the actual spectators, we see beyond a doubt that it is a regard for the judgment of the impartial spectator which most truly fits man for society. We must therefore look upon the "man within" not only as the embodiment of the norms of sympathy, but more concretely as the guardian of society's existence and welfare. The man within informs us not only that by certain actions we render ourselves subject to the indignation and contempt of mankind which usually follow such actions, but also that we have violated "those sacred rules, upon the tolerable observation of which depend the whole security and peace of human society."[18]

Thus the introduction of the impartial spectator is not the abandonment of the principle of sympathy, but its completion. Our moral judgments are based upon the organic unity of individuals in a social whole whose peace and security are of compelling importance. The compulsion which we find in the rules of morality belongs to them as the principles of existence of the social order. Clearly this does not introduce a contrary principle, such as the abstract reason of the intellectual school. There is introduced, indeed, an objectivity and a necessity into the moral laws, and Smith himself calls this objective element—the inner man—"reason." But the rationality which these laws possess is their relevancy to the demands of the "great fabric of human society," and they are far from being apprehended by a process of ratiocination. The individual moral consciousness has developed in an environment of

[17] *Loc. cit.*
[18] *Ibid.*, pt. iii, ch. 3.

moral approbation and disapprobation, and consists of a mass of social judgments appropriated by long association; and because the moral consciousness has been built up thus slowly and unconsciously, its deliverances are immediate and suffused with feeling. But at the same time the very existence of the moral consciousness involves the participation of the individual, to some degree at least, in the social consciousness. Far from abandoning the principles of the sentimental school, Adam Smith may be said to have given them for the first time a tenable philosophical basis.

One further criticism of Adam Smith's ethics needs to be considered. It has often been objected that in the theory of the *Moral Sentiments* those very moral feelings are assumed as necessarily existing before the sympathy in which they are said to originate. This objection serves to illustrate very clearly the contrast between Adam Smith's original conception and the customary point of view of the eighteenth century. As stated by Thomas Brown, it is as follows: "If we had not a principle of moral approbation . . . . the most exact sympathy of passions . . . . would have been a proof to us of an agreement of feelings, but of nothing more. It proves to us more, because the emotions, which we compare with our own, are recognized by us as moral feelings, independently of the mere agreement. We do not merely share the sentiments of the agent, but we share his moral sentiments, the recognition of which, as moral sentiments, has preceded our very sympathy."[19] This criticism fails to perceive that one purpose of Smith's inquiry is to describe the moral sentiments in their origin and development. There can be no doubt that for any individual the moral law is already in existence in the society into which he is born, and his individual sympathies are more or less regulated by that law, the "general rules" to which we have

[19] *Lectures*, IV, 86; cf. also IV, 99. Other criticisms to the same effect are found in Cousin, *op. cit.*, p. 177; Jouffroy, *op. cit.*, II, 27. Delatour has even gone to the length of misstating Smith's theory to fit the criticism: "Selon Smith, ce sentiment qui est en nous, sympathise avec tout ce qui est bien chez nos semblables et il est antipathique à toute vilaine action de leur part" (*op. cit.*, p. 88). No wonder he brings the criticism (p. 91): "La sympathie présuppose la loi morale, elle ne la constitue pas."

referred. But Smith is describing the growth of the moral sentiments from originally pre-moral elements. What he presupposes is not the moral law, but certain "original passions" which gradually grow into morality under the influence of the social principle. He does not clearly state what these primitive instincts are, sometimes regarding them as pleasure and pain, sometimes as gratitude and resentment; but he is clear that they develop into morality by means of the social principle which enables the individual to identify himself first with the welfare of his neighbors, and ultimately with that of all members of his society. Smith would never deny that the empirical facts of sympathy presuppose the moral law; what he intends to show is the dependence, in the last analysis, of the moral law upon the social principle, or sympathy. As a theory which recognizes development and growth, the *Moral Sentiments* is subject to all the criticisms which can be brought from the standpoint of a mechanical logic; but its very originality consists in having transcended the limitations of this formalistic logic.

If now we turn to the characteristic social problem of the eighteenth century—the problem of the origin and nature of society—the social implications of the doctrine of sympathy are shown more concretely. In contrast with the prevailing 'nominalism' of eighteenth-century social philosophy, the ethical theory of Adam Smith implies the existence of a social order possessing a natural and real unity. Smith goes farther than Hume in criticising the contract theory of society. For in spite of his criticisms of the crude form of that theory, Hume nevertheless regards the rules of justice, which make society possible, as possessing an artificial character; they are approved because they are perceived to be useful for the common welfare. Adam Smith opposes this conception of justice. If society is natural, our approbation of the rules of justice must also be natural. What is the basis of this approbation? Are the rules of justice approved of because we perceive their necessity for the existence of the social union from which we ourselves derive a benefit? Or does our approbation of the enforcement of justice occur prior to any reflection upon its useful effects? Smith upholds the latter point against Hume by two main arguments. The first is that, though injustice is destructive and justice is beneficial to society, "it is seldom this consideration which first animates us. . . . . All men, even the most stupid and unthinking, abhor fraud, perfidy, and injustice, and delight to see them punished. But few men have reflected upon the necessity of justice to the existence of society, how obvious soever that necessity may appear to be."[20] In the second place, the interest which we take in the persons immediately concerned in any act of justice or injustice is not a result of our interest in society, but is directed toward the acts themselves. "When a single man is injured, or destroyed, we demand the punishment of the wrong that has been done to him, not so much from a concern for the general interest of society, as from a concern for that very individual who has been injured." Although such instinctive and unreflective acts of approbation are exactly the acts which an enlightened consciousness of the social needs would cause the individual to perform, yet we are not to assume that it is the contrivance of man which has produced them. "When by natural principles we are led to advance those ends which a refined and enlightened reason would recommend to us, we are very apt to impute to that reason, as to their efficient cause, the sentiments and actions by which we advance those ends, and to imagine that to be the wisdom of man, which in reality is the wisdom of God."[21] In this one sentence Adam Smith has given expression to and shown the fallacy in the fundamental assumption of the social rationalism of the eighteenth century.

It must be admitted that Adam Smith is too much a man of his own century not to be impressed with the evidences of design in the universe. He sees that the social order is admirably contrived to serve all the needs of the individuals who compose it. Where he differs from his century is in denying that the rationality which the social order presents is per-

[20] *Moral Sentiments*, pt. ii, sec. ii, ch. 3.

[21] *Ibid.*, pt. ii, sec. ii, ch. 3.

fectly transparent to human reason. The foundations of society are not to be discovered in the rational or reflective experience of the individual, but in his instinctive life. The social order is a unity possessing its own laws above the devices of human reason. "The great, the immense fabric of human society, that fabric which to raise and support seems in this world, if I may say so, to have been the peculiar and darling care of Nature"[22]—this fabric is exquisitely adjusted, but not as a result of human contrivance. Some of the examples which Adam Smith gives to illustrate this realistic conception of society are significant because of their connection with his economic and political thought. Human reason would perhaps have suggested that the best way to equalize the necessaries of life would have been to divide the earth into equal portions among all its inhabitants. But by Providence the earth was divided among a few lordly masters, and these are "led by an invisible hand to make nearly the same distribution of the necessaries of life, which would have been made had the earth been divided into equal portions among all its inhabitants; and thus, without intending it, without knowing it, advance the interest of the society."[23] Again, rational reflection would tell us that kings are mere men, the servants of the people, to be obeyed or resisted as the public utility may require. But this is "the doctrine of reason and philosophy; . . . it is not the doctrine of Nature."[24] Adam Smith's reliance upon 'nature' and the 'invisible hand' is to be taken as more than a deistic faith in the harmony and beneficence of the universe. It is a recognition of the social order both as the complete expression of the individual life, and as an organic unity maintaining itself independently of the will of individuals. It is, moreover, a recognition that society is a great historical reality against which the wills of particular men, both in fact and by right, are relatively impotent to contend. He distrusts the "man of system" who attempts to "new-model the constitution, and to alter, in

[22] *Loc. cit.*
[23] *Ibid.*, pt. iv, ch. 1.
[24] *Ibid.*, pt. i, sec. iii, ch. 2.

some of its most essential parts, that system of government under which the subjects of a great empire have enjoyed, perhaps, peace, security, and even glory, during the course of several centuries together."[25] The true statesman and reformer "will respect the established powers and privileges even of individuals, and still more those of the great orders and societies, into which the state is divided." There breathes in these passages a spirit of political and social conservatism which contrasts markedly with the revolutionary philosophy of the latter half of the century; and which, as exemplified not only in Smith, but also in Hume and most of all in Burke, is but the outgrowth of the historical and anti-rationalistic tendencies which we have already noted in eighteenth-century thought.

How does such a political conservatism accord with Adam Smith's liberalism in economic theory? This question is a phase of the more general problem of relating the conception of society reached here at the end of the *Moral Sentiments* with the conception which meets us in the *Wealth of Nations*. We must postpone for the present the discussion of the details of this problem; but it is important to note here certain respects in which the two theories supplement one another. Both the *Moral Sentiments* and the *Wealth of Nations* assert that society is a real unity, a harmonious order of individuals. The *Moral Sentiments*, however, shows that this harmony between the interests of the various individuals and the interest of society is based upon the operation of the principle of sympathy; it is an internal harmony produced by the mutual adaptation of the individuals to one another on the basis of a free communication of sentiments. The social order therefore is intimately adapted to the interests of the individuals, and the individual is in turn the expression of the social environment in which he lives. As a product of the social experience the member of society is through and through social; his very interests are those which have been developed in him in the course of his experience in society. In a certain sense it can be said that the theory of sympathy

[25] *Op. cit.*, pt. vi, sec. ii.

in the *Moral Sentiments* is a necessary presupposition of the economic harmony exhibited in the *Wealth of Nations*. It is because he is social by nature that the individual, in pursuing his own interests, advances most advantageously the common welfare.

The principle of sympathy therefore involves theoretical consequences which go far beyond the ethical problems to which it was first applied. It gave rise to a tradition opposed to the rationalism of the eighteenth century, and tending toward a more concrete, a more historical, a more immanent and positive social philosophy. This opposition is evident in Adam Smith's own thought, and comes out most explicitly in the contrast recognized in the *Moral Sentiments* between the virtue of justice and the virtue of benevolence. The discussion of this ethical distinction in its wider implications will be the concern of the following chapter.

CHAPTER III.

JUSTICE VERSUS BENEVOLENCE.

A CERTAIN dualism appears in nearly all the moral sense theories of the nature of virtue. We have already referred to the incipient cleavage in Hutcheson's ethics between the virtue of self-interest and that of benevolence. Two of the best examples of the same tendency toward dualism are found in the ethical theories of Adam Smith's contemporaries, Hume and Lord Kames. Hume finds a difference in obligation between justice and the other virtues, and accounts for this difference by finding the origin of justice in an artifice or convention entered into for the utility of society, and supported in individual cases by sympathy with the welfare of the social whole; whereas the other virtues spring from sympathy with the happiness or misery of individuals. Each particular case of justice needs to be viewed as an instance of an approved general rule before the specific act can receive proper approbation; but in the case of the other virtues the individual act is judged immediately and upon its own merits.[1] The same distinction, with some modifications, is found in the ethical philosophy of Lord Kames.[2] Kames strenuously opposes the theory of the conventional nature of justice, and insists that its origin lies in a "natural sense of justice" rather than in a sympathy with the welfare of society, yet he retains virtually the same dualism when he distinguishes between 'primary' and 'secondary' virtues. The primary virtues are such virtues as justice and truth, which are more essential to the existence of society than the latter, and can be exacted as duties. The secondary virtues, while they receive greater approbation, can never have the obligation which the primary virtues imply. As for Adam Smith, we have already noted that he sets up a

[1] *Treatise*, II, 252 ff.

[2] *Essays on the Principles of Morality and Natural Religion*, 1751.

similar dualism: virtue he regards as twofold, consisting of self-interest regulated by justice, and the higher virtue of benevolence.

Whatever may have been the professed grounds of this dualism in the writers of the moral sense school, one most important determining factor was the difficulty of reconciling their central position with the recognition of the ethical value of the economic motive. During the two hundred years preceding the beginning of the eighteenth century, changes in the commercial and industrial situation had been imposing upon the other-worldly ideal of earlier centuries a radically different one, that of material prosperity. However much worldly goods may actually have been desired formerly, whether with good or bad conscience, it was only after the Renaissance that they were openly recognized as important elements in the sum total of values. Material prosperity was now valued for its own sake, and the 'worldly' ideal was openly accepted. The moving principle in the new era of material prosperity was self-assertion, not self-denial; and this implied an open break with the previous system of ethical standards. Mandeville, in his *Fable of the Bees*, set forth most strikingly this break with the ethics of the past involved in the new era of public prosperity based on individual initiative. Stripped of satire and affected paradox the central point of his contention was that if the material prosperity of England was the end desired, then the way to it was not over the medieval paths of self-denial—which he perversely persisted in making the whole of virtue—but through the activity of self-interest, in its various forms of pride, vanity, selfishness, luxury, and the like. These 'vices' were responsible for all the comforts of life which modern industry had provided. Without human desire—by which he meant in the main a 'rising standard of living'—progress was impossible either toward wealth or toward civilization.[3] Thus the dilemma was distinctly formulated: abandon the belief in the value of material prosperity, or recognize the worth of self-interest. For the moralists of the sentimental school this recognition was especially difficult;

[3] II, 302, 303.

for while the rationalists could justify the working of self-interest by an appeal to a rational or natural order of things in which this motive works for the welfare of the whole, it was difficult or dangerous to found upon the sentiments an approbation of selfishness. Thus the preceding moralists of this school either had denied the ethical value of self-interest, or if they recognized it, had been unable to make this recognition logically consistent with their more basic principles; and in Hume and Kames the outcome was an openly recognized dualism.

Adam Smith had also read the *Fable of the Bees*. He saw through the fallacy in Mandeville's paradox, but was also acute enough to realize that it "could never have imposed upon so great a number of persons, nor have occasioned so general an alarm among those who are the friends of better principles, had it not in some respects bordered upon the truth."[4] One of these respects, as we see in the *Wealth of Nations*, was the acceptance of self-interest as the driving force in the economic order. For this reason we should expect to find in the *Moral Sentiments* a recognition of the same principle. This is clearly the case. Smith's criticism of the ethical systems of the benevolent moralists was that they failed to account for the approbation of the inferior virtues of prudence, industry and frugality. "The care of the health, of the fortune, of the rank and reputation of the individual, the objects upon which his comfort and happiness in this life are supposed principally to depend, is considered as the proper business of that virtue which is commonly called prudence."[5] The characteristics of prudence are caution, sincerity, steady friendship, inoffensiveness, industry, frugality. "The prudent man is always both supported and rewarded by the entire approbation of the impartial spectator, and of the representative of the impartial spectator, the man within the breast."[6]

But Adam Smith was far from preaching a doctrine of unregulated self-interest. Where the pursuit of his own

[4] *Moral Sentiments*, pt. vii, sec. ii, ch. 4.

[5] *Ibid.*, pt. vi, sec. i.

[6] *Loc. cit.*

interest by one individual will result in injury to another, it cannot meet with the approbation of mankind. Such cases will be many, for every man is by nature more interested in his own concerns than in those of others. This distortion of reality because of his particular point of view is counteracted in his moral experience by an appeal to the impartial spectator. "When he views himself in the light in which he is conscious that others will view him, he sees that to them he is but one of the multitude in no respect better than any other in it. . . . . In the race for wealth, and honor, and preferments, he may run as hard as he can, and strain every nerve and every muscle, in order to outstrip all his competitors. But if he should jostle, or throw down any of them, the indulgence of the spectators is entirely at an end. It is a violation of fair play which they cannot admit of. This man is to them, in every respect as good as he: they do not enter into that self-love by which he prefers himself so much to this other, and cannot go along with the motive from which he hurt him."[7] Justice, therefore, is the principle of fair play. Smith sometimes calls it negative beneficence, since it consists in refraining from injury to others. It is the objective point of view from which all individuals are alike, each one entitled to as much consideration as another.

But although self-interest regulated by justice is recognized as an essential element in virtue, yet there are other and nobler virtues. These are the positively beneficent ones, such as generosity, charity, benevolence, pity and the like. They are characterized by the fact that their observance brings greater approbation than does the observance of the inferior virtues. This follows in part from their dependence upon the free will of the individual. Their reward is not the indirect approbation of mankind as shown in legal immunity, but the direct approbation of humanity and the inner consciousness of merit—a qualitatively different sanction. The punishment which follows the violation of these virtues is not the indirect disapprobation of legal condemnation, but the direct aversion and dislike of our fellow-men, and added to this, our own

[7] *Op. cit.*, pt. ii, sec. ii, ch. 2.

inner sense of remorse and unworthiness. Thus the sanctions of the higher virtues are on a qualitatively different plane. For acts of justice, the sanction is traditional, stereotyped, generalized approbation and disapprobation; but in the case of benevolent actions, the agent appeals to the very source of the moral world and gets his verdict in each individual case upon its merits.

The emphasis upon these as the superior virtues, even as virtue *par excellence*, may seem to introduce a difficulty into Adam Smith's system by denying the previous recognition of self-interest as a justifiable motive of action. It seems that we have reverted after all to the benevolent theory, and that an action is really virtuous only when its aim is the happiness or welfare of others. Thus, in spite of his criticism of the benevolent moralists, Adam Smith's system would seem to be scarcely distinguishable from theirs. Self-interest and altruism are not different degrees of the same impulse, but opposite impulses. They cannot exist side by side; if one rules, the other must abdicate. Hence to call one inferior to another is tantamount to the denial of its right to rule at all. Consequently the theory of sympathy, in spite of its insistence upon self-interest, would be thus reduced to the same doctrine of benevolence which Hutcheson had maintained. Nor is it possible to save the situation by prescribing certain spheres of activity for the two virtues, the 'economic world' for the inferior virtues of self-interest, and the world of more intimate relationships for the higher virtues.[8] This is merely paralleling our theoretical difficulty with another difficulty in the world of actual relationships. The economic world and the ethical world are not mutually exclusive, and we can accept such an artificial division only if no other interpretation of Adam Smith is possible.

The difficulty can be avoided, I think, by a different reading of the contrast between justice and beneficence. Does Adam Smith mean by benevolence merely what Hutcheson meant by the same term, and is the contrast between self-interest

[8] As is done, for example, by Zeyss, *Adam Smith und der Eigennutz.*

and benevolence properly expressed by the antithesis between egoism and altruism?

There are two main respects, according to Adam Smith, in which justice differs from the virtues of beneficence. In the first place, we may properly use force to prevent the injury of one man by another, but we can hardly attempt to enforce by legal sanctions the virtues of charity and benevolence. The virtues of positive benevolence are left to the freedom of the individual. Sometimes, indeed, a sovereign may properly prescribe certain duties of beneficence to his subjects, in addition to the duties of justice, but the degree to which that can be ventured is one of the most delicate questions in legislation, and in general may be said to be impossible. The possibility of attaching legal sanctions to the rules of justice leads us to the second point of difference. Justice is distinguished from benevolence by the fact that it can be treated with scientific exactness. The rules of justice constitute the civil and criminal law of states; and the "principles upon which those rules either are, or ought to be founded, are the subject of a particular science, of all sciences by far the most important, but hitherto, perhaps, the least cultivated, that of natural jurisprudence."[9] In the *Moral Sentiments* Adam Smith contents himself with general mention of the science of jurisprudence and does not attempt to carry it into details; that, he promises, is to be the substance of another work which he intends to give to the public. "I shall in another discourse endeavor to give an account of the general principles of law and government, and of the different revolutions they have undergone in the different ages and periods of society, not only in what concerns justice, but in what concerns police, revenue, and arms, and whatever else is the object of law. I shall not, therefore, at present enter into any further detail concerning the history of jurisprudence."[10] In contrast with the precision of the rules of justice, the other virtues are less precisely determinable. "The rules of justice may be compared to the rules of grammar; the rules of the other virtues,

[9] *Moral Sentiments*, pt. vi., sec. ii, Introd.
[10] *Ibid., ad fin.*

to the rules which critics lay down for the attainment of what is sublime and elegant in composition. The one are precise, accurate and indispensable. The other are loose, vague and indeterminate, and present us rather with a general idea of the perfection we ought to aim at, than afford us any certain and infallible directions for acquiring it."[11]

The importance of this distinction between jurisprudence and ethics becomes clear when it is seen that for Adam Smith the field of jurisprudence included the study of "what concerns police, revenue and arms," in other words, the economic and political phenomena studied in the *Wealth of Nations*. Thus the distinction between justice and benevolence, between jurisprudence and ethics, is not peculiar to the moral theory but extends throughout Adam Smith's philosophy. The dualism of virtues seems to imply a dualism of social phenomena, some capable of exact rules, and others whose principles can be understood only in the large. To the former class evidently belong the exact inquiries of the projected work on jurisprudence and of the *Wealth of Nations*; to the latter group the specifically ethical phenomena treated of in the *Moral Sentiments*. What is the relation between these two groups of facts? This is the most fundamental question in Adam Smith's philosophy, and its solution is necessary for an understanding of the relation of his economic theory to his general philosophy of society.

The recognition of this as the fundamental problem enables us to see the inadequacy of merely showing that the *Wealth of Nations* does not presuppose a different set of virtues from those of the *Moral Sentiments*. In reality this supposed solution only carries the problem one step farther back, and we see that its source lies in the *Moral Sentiments* itself. The question of the relation of economic theory to social philosophy is to be solved only by understanding the relation between the inferior economic virtues and the other virtues, less accurately definable, but more significant for ethical theory.

The best approach to the problem of understanding the relation of these two sets of virtues will be gained by examining the theory of jurisprudence. Although Adam Smith's work

[11] *Op. cit.*, pt. iii, ch. 6.

on jurisprudence was never completed, and the materials which he had collected were burned by his own hand before his death, we are able to understand its general nature from the notes of his *Lectures*, and from the hints in the *Moral Sentiments*. The last section of the latter work, which is in a sense a transition to the proposed work on jurisprudence, makes clear that what the author is contemplating is "a system of what might properly be called natural jurisprudence, or a theory of the general principles which ought to run through and be the foundation of the laws of all nations."[12] Grotius, he says in conclusion, is the first who has attempted to construct such a system. The same viewpoint is stated in his *Lectures*. Jurisprudence is there defined as "that science which inquires into the general principles which ought to be the foundation of the laws of all nations." Next follow short discussions of Hobbes, Pufendorf and the Baron de Cocceii; beyond these, he says, there are no systems of note upon this subject.[13] The scope of jurisprudence is next outlined; it includes: (1) the principles of justice, whose aim is the security of individuals; (2) the principles of police, or public security, cleanliness and opulence; (3) the principles of public revenues; (4) the self-protecting function of the state, or "arms"; and (5) the laws of nations. An examination of these lecture notes shows that parts (2) and (3) correspond to the ground later covered by the economic inquiries of the *Wealth of Nations*.

Without going into a detailed examination of these lectures we can see that the basis of the theory of jurisprudence is the Roman *jus gentium* and *jus naturale*, revived by Grotius and Pufendorf in the preceding century. When therefore Adam Smith speaks of the scientific character of the rules of justice and identifies them with a science little cultivated but vastly important, we know beyond a doubt that these rules of justice are based upon the 'natural law' of seventeenth-century thought. It is also easy to understand why he regarded these inquiries as possessing an exact character. The doctrine of natural law was a statement of the universal relations of

[12] *Loc. cit.*
[13] *Lectures*, p. 1.

men considered as reasonable and social beings. No attempt was made to define the individual further than as a rational and responsible unit of the social order (considered in its widest sense), and as the repository of rights and duties of various kinds. These rights and duties were derived from the most common relations of human life, those relations which can be assumed with more or less generality of all individuals. Each human being possesses certain rights as a man, certain others as a member of a family, still others as a citizen of a state.[14] This system of natural law dealt only with the externals of human life; the inner world of values and motives was not considered except as it expressed itself in outward acts. Humanity was an aggregation of isolated elements whose relations could be cast into legal moulds. In such an order of society it is possible to have exactness for the mere reason that differences are ignored. The scientific accuracy of rational jurisprudence is attained only by neglecting the characteristics which give each individual instance its significance and value.

The central assumptions of the theory of natural law are therefore directly at variance with the principles developed in Adam Smith's ethical theory. The natural law assumes that the individual is ultimate, an underived and irreducible unit of the social order, whereas the doctrine of sympathy as employed by Smith exhibits the individual coming to himself through his social relations. The natural law regards humanity as an assemblage of identical units; whereas Smith's moral theory makes room for all the variety of individual character and experience. The one is a legal point of view, based upon an abstract individualism, the other is a philosophical theory which denies the validity of this abstract individualism in

[14] Introducing the subject of Justice, Smith distinguishes the ways in which a man may be injured; i.e. as a man, as a member of a family, or as a member of a state; and based on this is the threefold division of jurisprudence into public, domestic and private jurisprudence. Under the head of public jurisprudence he deals with the rights of sovereign and subjects, the basis of citizenship, and the principles underlying the political union. Under domestic law are considered the relations of husband and wife, parent and child, master and servant, guardian and ward; and under private law, the acquisition of property, contracts, privileges and mortgages. *Op. cit., passim.*

the moral experience. The ethical dualism found in Hume and Kames points, at least by implication, toward the same recognition of the insufficiency of the legal point of view. The contrast they make between justice and the other virtues is ostensibly a contrast between two kinds of moral actions, but in reality they are asserting the inadequacy of justice alone to provide the basis for an ethical theory. When Hume calls justice an artificial virtue, he exhibits his philosophical dissatisfaction with the legalistic standpoint. Kames's admission that justice is more necessary and more obligatory, while benevolence receives greater approbation, shows his confusion of the legal with the philosophical standpoint, but indicates at the same time his perception of the inadequacy of the former point of view to describe the concrete realities of the moral life. Similarly when Adam Smith brings forward the same contrast between justice and benevolence, it is not simply a contrast between two different kinds of moral action —i.e. negative and positive beneficence—but a contrast between two different theoretical points of view. An abstract individualism, proper enough in the discussion of legal relations, is inadequate to express the higher realities of the individual moral experience.

In the light of this anticipatory interpretation, let us examine in more detail the emphasis which Smith places upon the moral superiority of benevolence. "The man who acts according to the rules of perfect prudence, of strict justice, and of proper benevolence, may be said to be perfectly virtuous."[15] This is Adam Smith's picture of the ideal man. But since benevolence cannot be guided by rules, what is the criterion of *proper benevolence?* We must appeal here again to Adam Smith's equivalent of Aristotle's *ὁ φρόνιμος*. Only the "men of happiest mould" are able to suit always the proper degree of benevolence to the object, and they are able to do so, by an appeal, not to their own interests, but to the impartial spectator and his sympathies. Since the impartial spectator is the repository of the social demands, it would seem that by these "men of happiest mould" Adam Smith means those

[15] *Moral Sentiments*, pt. vi, sec. iii.

who are most responsive to the judgment of their social milieu, those who are most sensitive to the organic unity of human society. If this is the case, then the highest virtue is the possession in the highest degree of the ability to participate sympathetically in the feelings and sentiments of humanity. The better the individual, the greater his sensitiveness to the social consciousness.[16] The degree of an individual's excellence depends upon the degree of his responsiveness to his human environment, present, past and future, ranging all the way from the unconcern of the merely just man, who obeys the rules of justice because of their external sanctions, to the man of complete sympathy who can see all things, as it were, *sub specie societatis*.

Almost the entire section which Adam Smith devotes to the discussion of the contrast between justice and benevolence is given over to a description of the successive stages by which the social consciousness develops, and the individual passes beyond the mechanical relations of the plane of justice to an appreciation of his membership in the great society of humanity.[17] The guiding thread in the discussion is the principle that personal contact is the basis of the social consciousness. There is no mysterious affinity between human beings from the mere fact of their humanity, no love for humanity in general. The individual is brought out of himself by his sympathetic participation in the sentiments and affections of other individuals with whom he associates. Those whom he knows in the family circle are naturally the objects of his first and deepest sympathies. The social consciousness thus begun in the family group grows as his sympathies spread out in widening circles, first to his clan or neighborhood, then to his nation, and finally to the whole system of the universe. Nature has so established the order of our sympathies that those individuals who are in a position to be most benefited by our good offices shall be the first to receive our sympathies. The same principle holds true with respect to the societies which we support. "The state or sovereignty in which we

[16] *Op. cit.*, pt. iii, ch. 2.
[17] *Ibid.*, pt. vi, sec. ii.

have been born and educated, and under the protection of which we continue to live, is, in ordinary cases, the greatest society upon whose happiness or misery, our good or bad conduct can have much influence. It is accordingly, by nature, most strongly recommended to us."[18] But the state itself is a group of societies, each possessing a life of its own and an instinct for self-maintenance, and the mutual adjustment of these orders and societies gives the state its constitution. Each individual endeavors to secure the aggrandizement of his own group and to help it to resist the encroachment of others. None of these groups is self-sufficient, however, and the interplay of them all with one another is necessary in the harmonious ordering of the state. It is because he is a member of many such groups that the complexity of the individual's life arises, for countless combinations of sympathies may be influencing him at any given moment. The different nations are in turn subordinated to the universal society of humanity, and a sympathy with this universal society is an even higher stage of the moral consciousness. Moreover, the sympathies of the individual extend even beyond the society of nations; eventually he may become consciously a member of the universal society of all rational beings. Just as the wise and virtuous man is willing that his own interests be sacrificed to the public welfare of his own particular order and society, and in turn is willing that the interest of that order should give way to the greater interest of the state of which it is a part; he should also be willing that those great concerns themselves be sacrified to the superior ends of the universe, considered as a society of all sensible and intelligent beings, under the administration and direction of God himself. Though that order is beyond the reach of our good efforts, the contemplation of it is the most sublime achievement of the human spirit.

This exposition of the development of the moral consciousness suggests that the observance of the rules of justice is the minimum basis upon which society can exist; at this stage individuals are mutually isolated and brought into adjustment

[18] *Op. cit.*, pt. vi, sec. ii, ch. 2.

only by external authority; the social union is upheld by a general sense of its utility and a "mercenary exchange of good offices according to an agreed valuation." But the higher stage of society is one in which there is perfect consciousness on the part of each member of the rôle which he is playing in the social order,—the society in which each individual is able to rise above his own particularity and view all his actions and interests in the light of the spiritual unity of humanity.

Interpreted in this sense, the virtues of beneficence are merely a more explicit recognition of the organic relation of an individual to his fellow-men. They represent the individual become conscious of his membership in the social order. The man who merely obeys the rules of justice—who needs rules—is not conscious of the social implications of his own individuality; he acts blindly and mechanically. Law is for him an alien thing which coerces to the performance of acts which are beneficial to the whole, but which, from his individual standpoint, are the exactions of tyranny. On the other hand, the superior man equally follows the rules of justice, but they are not coercive, for he has that within himself which is greater than laws; he communicates with the social mind where the rules of justice have their source, and does freely what the inferior man must be compelled to do. It is not adequate, therefore, to represent the passage from the lower to the higher virtues as the passage from egoism to altruism. The inferior virtues, i.e. self-interest restrained by justice, are in a very great degree social, for upon the free play of individual interests depends the material welfare of society. The selfish individual is really serving social ends, though his service is unconscious. Nor do the higher virtues exclude self-interest; the perfectly virtuous man must preserve his own welfare, but he does it conscious of the relation of his own welfare to the good of the whole, and he needs no restraining hand of the law to tell him when his own interests must be sacrificed. The lower and the higher virtues are not opposed to one another, but are thoroughly in accord; they represent, not different kinds of actions, but different levels of the social consciousness.

This I take to be the real meaning of Adam Smith's dualism of virtues. Any other interpretation would introduce intolerable inconsistencies, and would inevitably result either in a denial of the validity of self-interest and the consequent classification of Smith as merely a follower of Hutcheson, or in a reduction of the benevolent virtues to the self-regarding ones, a reflected egoism. But if we make the difference between the lower and the higher virtues a difference in the degree of the operation of sympathy—an interpretation thoroughly in accord with the spirit of the system—there is no necessity for distorting either the egoistic or the altruistic element in the ethical theory. The two are only different phases in the individual mind of the social principle which produces both.

The dualism of virtues, therefore, corresponds to a distinction fundamental in Adam Smith's thought—the distinction between jurisprudence and ethics; and the superior excellence ascribed to beneficence in contrast with justice is an assertion of the insufficiency of legal conceptions as a basis for ethical and social philosophy. The legal point of view posits individuals as given in their isolation and blank similarity; the doctrine of sympathy shows that this isolation and similarity are assumed, not found, and perceives the steps by which from mere particularity the individual progresses to universality by sympathetic association with his kind. From the one standpoint, society is an association of isolated individuals, identical in nature, brought together by an external tie, and interacting more or less mechanically with one another. Their interest is simply a "mercenary exchange of good offices"; they are unconscious of the social mind in which they live and move. From the higher standpoint, these same facts are transformed and given a more concrete expression in socially conscious personalities.

CHAPTER IV.

THE ECONOMIC ORDER.

A CURSORY examination of the *Wealth of Nations* shows that its inquiry is not restricted to what would to-day be regarded as economic facts. This has given rise to the oft-repeated statement that the work is not primarily an economic treatise, but a broad study in social welfare. Comte, among others, has asserted that Adam Smith merely proposed "to illustrate some leading points of social philosophy by luminous analyses relating to the division of employments, the function of money, the general action of banks, etc., and other chief portions of the industrial developments of the human race."[1] The belief that the *Wealth of Nations* is primarily a sociological rather than an economic inquiry has been strangely supported by appealing to the fact that it is only a part of a larger study of social life which Adam Smith intended to write. This fact, however, points rather to the opposite conclusion. The *Wealth of Nations* is not itself the comprehensive work which Adam Smith had in mind, but only a limited part of it; and while we may admit that his range of interests included the whole field of social phenomena, we are forced to conclude that the *Wealth of Nations* is an expression of only a limited part of those interests.

The best way to understand the scope of the inquiry undertaken in the *Wealth of Nations* is to take the author's own statement of the matter. It will be remembered that he considered political economy as a branch of the science of jurisprudence, and therefore as belonging to that part of moral philosophy which he declared capable of exact treatment, as distinct from the philosophical and ethical questions treated in the *Moral Sentiments*. The nature and the scope of his investigation are stated explicitly in the *Wealth of Nations*. "The great object

[1] *Positive Philosophy*, II, 51-52, Martineau's translation.

of the political economy of every country is to increase the riches and power of that country."[2] Again: "Political economy, considered as a branch of the science of a statesman or legislator, proposes two distinct objects: first, to provide a plentiful revenue or subsistence for the people, or more properly to enable them to provide such a revenue or subsistence for themselves; and secondly, to supply the state or commonwealth with a revenue sufficient for the public services. It proposes to enrich both the people and the sovereign."[3] Comparison of this passage with the lectures on jurisprudence shows that the *Wealth of Nations* is the development of parts two and three of his lectures; the former covering the "principles of police, or public security, cleanliness and opulence"; the latter, "the principles of public revenues."[4] Political economy therefore is an exact science; it is that branch of jurisprudence which treats of the material welfare of political societies, under the twofold aspect of private and public wealth.

In order to test this tentative conception of the nature of Adam Smith's economic inquiry, let us examine the general plan of the *Wealth of Nations*, confining our attention to the points of philosophical importance. The specific economic doctrines will be discussed only as they have a bearing upon Adam Smith's general method and presuppositions.

The inquiry opens with the statement that the wealth of a nation consists in the annual product of the nation's labor; and that in consequence a country is more or less prosperous according to the productivity of its labor in proportion to the number of inhabitants. The means to the increase of national wealth is the improvement of the productive powers of labor. The industry of advanced societies is much more productive than that of ancient times and of uncivilized countries, and Smith points out as its cause the simple fact of the division of labor, which by increasing the skill and dexterity of each laborer increases the total product. This division of labor arises from a propensity in human nature to exchange, an

[2] *Wealth of Nations*, ed. Cannan, I, 351.
[3] *Ibid.*, I, 395.
[4] Cf. *supra*, p. 52.

instinct to barter; and is kept in existence by the impulse which leads each man to seek his own interest. From the division of labor spring a host of social activities. The exchange of products necessitates the use of money, and introduces all the facts of value and price as market expressions of the underlying labor value, modified in advanced societies by the share which belongs to land and capital as coöperating factors in production. The discussion of all the later chapters in the first book centers about price facts: the distinction between real and nominal price, natural and market price, the various component parts of price, the conditions which determine the wages of labor, the profits of capital stock, and the rent of land, with long digressions on the variations in the value of silver during the preceding four centuries, and the effects of the progress of improvement upon wages, rents, and the prices of various classes of products.

Book II, following the quest for the laws governing the productivity of human labor, recognizes that the division of labor must be supplemented by the accumulation of capital, and that the development of the one must go hand in hand with the increase of the other. This book, therefore, is concerned with the nature, the means of accumulation, and the employment of capital. The price facts which dominate the first book are equally the center of importance here. Capital is that part of the wealth of a society which is devoted to instruments of production; it has its origin in the savings of individuals, and these savings themselves are the result of the same self-interested instinct which gives rise to the division of labor. The various kinds of capital are then discussed, the characteristics of money and credit as a special kind of capital, the conditions governing the rate of interest, and the different ways in which capital may be employed in production.

Book III turns from the theoretical discussion of the factors that make for the increase of national wealth, and investigates the rise and effect of these factors in the industrial history of Europe. After a discussion of what would be the natural progress of opulence in civilized countries if left to follow its own course, Adam Smith shows that the natural order has been inverted as a result of historical conditions. Agriculture should, in the natural course of things, contribute the greatest share to public prosperity, and should be in a state of advancement superior to that of industry and commerce; but historical conditions growing out of the break-up of the Roman Empire and the subsequent fortunes of Europe have prevented the advancement of agriculture, chiefly by restrictions upon the freedom of individual enterprise, and have given a correspondingly greater importance to the industry and commerce of the towns. This book is a genuine contribution to the history of European civilization, for a study of the historical conditions which have affected the industrial development of Europe leads the author into a general discussion of medieval life and government.

If Book III may be called a contribution to economic history, Book IV is an attempt toward a history of economics. Adam Smith divided previous political economists into two classes, according as they have held that commerce or agriculture is the best way of enriching a people. Book IV deals at length with the principles of these two systems of political economy. Smith finds nothing to support in the mercantile system. He shows the fallacy in its policy of accumulating gold, and in the principles by which that policy was justified; and he insists that absolute freedom of trade would be far more productive of national wealth. This part of the book has remained ever since the arsenal of free-trade arguments. The specific regulations resorted to in the administration of the mercantile policy are considered at length and their defects exposed. In the course of the argument a wide range of social facts is covered. While the mercantile policy was altogether erroneous, Adam Smith finds that the Physiocratic or agricultural system is "the nearest approximation to the truth that has yet been published upon the subject of political economy."[5] He finds it at fault in representing the labor employed upon land as the only productive labor, but accepts its two contentions against the mercantile system, that wealth consists not in gold but in consumable

[5] *Op. cit.*, II, 176.

goods, and that perfect liberty is the only effectual expedient for increasing national wealth.

These four books have dealt with the first aim of political economy, that of providing a plentiful subsistence for the people; the last book deals with the question of supplying the state with a revenue sufficient for the public services. The system of natural liberty once established, the duties of the state will be restricted to defending the society against external aggression, to administering justice, and maintaining certain public works which it is not to the interest of any private individual to construct. Adam Smith here undertakes a historical examination of each of these functions of government, and, as in Book III, the inquiry leads him into all phases of the history of civilization. He shows the different measures of defense adopted by various nations, and the necessity of a standing army in an advanced society. He examines the history of the judicial system, especially as developed in England, and explains the separation of the judicial and the executive functions of government. The historical inquiry is meant to throw light upon the extent to which the expenses of these institutions should be defrayed by the society. The principle laid down is that each individual should pay in proportion to the benefit he derives from the institution under consideration, and only when the benefit goes to the whole society should the government bear the expense. The same principle is applied to public works, commercial companies, the universities, and the churches. The necessary expenses of the state having been ascertained, the available sources of public revenue are examined. Here there are two questions to be answered with regard to each revenue measure. Since justice demands that payment should be taken from individuals only in proportion to benefit received, it is necessary to determine the incidence of the taxes under examination. Since the government demands an adequate revenue, the next question is whether the proposed taxes will yield a revenue proportioned to the inconvenience and expense of collecting them. The remainder of the book is devoted to a discussion of various forms of taxation in the light of these two questions.

What now is the specific character of the inquiry conducted in the *Wealth of Nations?* In the first place, the *Wealth of Nations* must be regarded as an examination of the whole extent of social facts. There is nothing in the phenomena of human association which is excluded from its survey. It does not confine itself to a particular set of phenomena which are 'economic,' nor a particular set of activities called 'wealth-getting'; there is no such division of social facts in Adam Smith's mind. Equally clear, however, is it that it treats of social facts from a specific point of view, it examines them in a definite and limited connection. The inquiry into the facts of feudal institutions has a bearing upon the question of the industrial development of modern societies. The history of the temporal power of the church and the crisis of the Reformation are cited, not for their intrinsic value, but because of their relation to the question of collective expenditure. The effects of sea coast upon civilization, the rise of coined money, the history of the institution of a standing army, the origin of science among the Greeks, the history of education in medieval times, the growth of public debts in modern societies, the double code of morality current in civilized countries, the modes of electing bishops in the ancient Roman church—all these facts are cited because they are relevant to a specific purpose. The general aspect under which all social phenomena are considered is that of material well-being. Everything from the rate of exchange to the decisions of ecclesiastical councils has, according to Smith, a bearing upon the material welfare of a nation. This order of social phenomena considered as a system of wealth-producing factors is the economic order. It is not to be considered as apart from the moral order, a world of impersonal relations set off by itself; this is not Adam Smith's idea. The economic order is coextensive with the moral order; it *is* the social order considered as a wealth-producing system. The *Wealth of Nations,* therefore, surveys the whole field of social facts; it studies these facts, however, not for their intrinsic significance, but for their bearing upon the question of industrial prosperity.

Further examination will show that this order of social phenomena considered as a system of wealth-producing factors is explained by the existence and operation of a single human trait, self-interest. "The natural effort which every man is continually making to better his own condition"[6] is the principle which keeps the economic mechanism in activity. "The uniform, constant, and uninterrupted effort of every man to better his condition," is "the principle from which public and national, as well as private opulence is originally derived."[7] The relation of individuals to one another is based purely upon calculations of profit and loss. "Man has almost constant occasion for the help of his brethren, and it is in vain for him to expect it from their benevolence only. He will be more likely to prevail if he can interest their self-love in his favor, and show them that it is for their own advantage to do for him what he requires of them. Whoever offers to another a bargain of any kind, proposes to do this: Give me that which I want, and you shall have this which you want, is the meaning of every such offer; and it is in this manner that we obtain from one another the far greater part of those good offices which we stand in need of. It is not from the benevolence of the butcher, the brewer, or the baker, that we expect our dinner, but from their regard to their own interest. We address ourselves, not to their humanity, but to their self-love, and never talk to them of our own necessities but of their advantages."[8]

To show that Adam Smith's economic analysis rests in its fundamentals upon the motive of self-interest, we need only examine the system in the large. The two main causes of the productivity of modern industry are the division of labor and the accumulation of capital—the key facts in Books I and II respectively. Now it is the principle of self-interest in the individual which explains each of these facts. The individual finds it more to his interest to exercise his strength and develop his skill in one occupation and exchange the surplus of what he produces for the products of other men's skill, than to attempt to supply all his various needs by the labor of his own hands. Thus by following his own interest, so far as he understands it,

[6] *Op. cit.*, II, 172.
[7] *Ibid.*, I, 325.
[8] *Ibid.*, I, 16.

he is furthering the progress of his neighbors toward wealth and prosperity. Similarly the accumulation of capital needs no other explaining cause than self-interest. "The principle which prompts to save, is the desire of bettering our condition, a desire which, though generally calm and dispassionate, comes with us from the womb, and never leaves us till we go into the grave. In the whole interval which separates those two moments, there is scarce perhaps a single instant in which any man is so perfectly and completely satisfied with his situation, as to be without any wish of alteration or improvement of any kind."[9] While the opposite tendency to extravagance also exists in individuals, prudence and frugality are far more common; so that a nation can never be brought to bankruptcy except by public prodigality and imprudence. Even that must be carried to great excess before it will counteract the effects of individual saving. In spite of a great deal of public confusion and extravagance in England between 1660 and 1776, the capital of the nation steadily increased from the savings of individuals.

The same principle is the foundation of the theoretical discussion of Book V. It is assumed that the state is a coöperative association from which each individual wishes to derive as much benefit as possible, and to which he wishes to contribute as little as possible.[10] The justice of a system of taxation lies in the proportionality of the contribution exacted from the individual to the benefit he derives from the government. The question in each case is, Who is compelled to pay the tax? Evidently the whole discussion of the incidence of taxation proceeds on the assumption that no individual will pay a tax if he can by any means pass it on to his neighbors —either by raising rents, or the prices of the articles he sells, or his own wages. The problem of incidence is based entirely on the assumption of ruthless competition among all the individuals of the society.[11]

We have seen that the main doctrines of each of the theoreti-

[9] *Op. cit.*, I, 323-324.
[10] *Ibid.*, II, 310-312.
[11] *Ibid.*, II, 337-338, 340, 342, 355, 379, 381, *et al.*

cal books is based upon self-interest as the sole explanatory principle. This scarcely gives an idea, however, of the extent to which the principle is employed in the detailed working out of the system. Directly growing out of the division of labor are all the phenomena of exchange. Prudence gives rise to the invention of money, and money facilitates the working of the competitive principle.[12] All the explanations of price assume that no individual will pay more than is necessary for what he wants, and no one will sell for less than he can get; the higgling of such self-interested individuals establishes the prices of labor, rent and commodities. In the fixation of wages "the workmen desire to get as much, the masters to give as little as possible."[13] The profits of stock are regulated by the competitive principle; each merchant will turn his stock into that business which will bring him greatest return, and is always ready to take advantage of any opportunity to lower his costs and increase his sales.[14] The rate of interest is determined by the competition of borrowers.[15] Actual variations from uniformity in wages and profits are explained as factors tending to counterbalance the other advantages and disadvantages of the employments in which they are engaged. Freedom of competition brings about an equality in the whole of the advantages and disadvantages of the various employments.[16] Only by the freedom of labor to compete with itself is it possible that the industry of the society can be directed into the most beneficial channels. As for rent, "in adjusting the terms of the lease, the landlord endeavors to leave him [the tenant] no greater share of the produce than what is sufficient to keep up the stock from which he furnishes the seed, pays the labor, and purchases and maintains the cattle and other instruments of husbandry, together with the ordinary profits of farming stock in the neighborhood." The rent is therefore "the highest the tenant can afford to pay in the actual circumstances of the land."[17]

[12] *Op. cit.*, I, 24.
[13] *Ibid.*, I, 68.
[14] *Ibid.*, I, 89, 95.
[15] *Ibid.*, I, 97.
[16] *Ibid.*, I, 116.
[17] *Ibid.*, I, 145.

The employment of savings in production is likewise the effect of self-interest.[18] He who has more capital than he needs for immediate consumption naturally seeks to derive an additional revenue from its investment in some profitable occupation. He will invest his stock in that employment which will bring him most money, and that will be in the production of those goods for which there is the greatest demand. Thus the industrial mechanism is quickened in that part in which the need is greatest. Free competition in banks is advantageous to the public; it has resulted in the invention of bank-notes and the credit mechanism, and the other banking devices which have released a greater supply of capital for purposes of trade.[19] The interest of traders in turn gives occasion for foreign exchange.

It is when we find the competitive principle introduced as an explanation of many facts usually regarded as outside the sphere of economic rivalry that we see the thoroughgoing use which Adam Smith makes of the principle of self-interest. "The present admirable constitution of the courts of justice in England" is the result of the ancient system of maintaining them by fees collected from the parties at law; "each court endeavored, by superior dispatch and impartiality, to draw to itself as many cases as it could."[20] The corruption of law language is to be ascribed to economic causes. "It has been the custom in modern Europe to regulate, upon most occasions, the payment of the attorneys and clerks of court, according to the number of pages which they had occasion to write; the court, however, requiring that each page should contain so many lines, and each line so many words. In order to increase their payment, the attorneys and clerks have continued to multiply words beyond all necessity."[21] Like law courts, educational institutions owe their efficiency to competition. Great endowments for schools and colleges have diminished the necessity for application on the part of the teachers. "It is

[18] *Op. cit.*, I, 261.
[19] *Ibid.*, I, 276.
[20] *Ibid.*, II, 212.
[21] *Ibid.*, II, 213.

the interest of every man to live as much at his ease as he can; and if his emoluments are to be precisely the same, whether he does or does not perform some very laborious duty, it is certainly his interest, at least as interest is vulgarly understood, either to neglect it altogether, or, if he is subject to some authority which will not suffer him to do this, to perform it in as careless and slovenly a manner as that authority will permit. If he is naturally active and a lover of labor, it is his interest to employ that activity in any way, from which he can derive some advantage, rather than in the performance of his duty, from which he can derive none."[22] The ancient Greek teachers form a striking contrast to the lecturers in the English universities, for the interests of the former depended upon the number of pupils they could attract by their talents; "and the emulation which an unrestrained competition never fails to excite, appears to have brought that talent to a very high degree of perfection."[23]

The church and the clergy are not exempt from the same iron law of self-interest. The clergy "may either depend altogether for their subsistence upon the voluntary contributions of their hearers; or they may derive it from some other fund to which the law of their country may entitle them. . . . Their exertion, their zeal and industry, are likely to be much greater in the former situation than in the latter. . . . In the Church of Rome, the industry and zeal of the inferior clergy are kept more alive by the powerful motive of self-interest, than perhaps in any established Protestant church."[24] The solidarity of the temporal power of the pope in medieval times was due to the fact that he had the disposal of the benefices; so "the grossest delusions of superstition were supported in such a manner by the private interests of so great a number of people as put them out of all danger from any assault of human reason."[25] Ever since the sovereigns of France and England have succeeded in depriving the pope of the disposal of the great

[22] *Op. cit.*, II, 250.
[23] *Ibid.*, II, 265.
[24] *Ibid.*, II, 273-274.
[25] *Ibid.*, II, 287.

benefices, the clergy of those countries have been less devoted. "The clergy of France have in general shown less respect to the decrees of the papal court than the clergy of any other Catholic country. In all the disputes which their sovereign has had with the pope, they have almost constantly taken party with the former. This independency of the clergy of France upon the court of Rome, seems to be principally founded upon the Pragmatic Sanction and the Concordat. In the earlier periods of the monarchy, the clergy of France appear to have been as much devoted to the pope as those of any other country."[26]

One of the great humanitarian movements of modern times, the abolition of slavery, is explained in the same terms. "The experience of all ages and nations, I believe, demonstrates that the work done by slaves, though it appears to cost only their maintenance, is in the end the dearest of any. A person who can acquire no property, can have no other interest but to eat as much, and to labor as little as possible. Whatever work he does beyond what is sufficient to purchase his own maintenance, can be squeezed out of him by violence only, and not by any interest of his own. . . . The planting of sugar and tobacco can afford the expense of slave cultivation. The raising of corn, it seems, in the present times, cannot. In the English colonies, of which the principal produce is corn, the far greater part of the work is done by freemen. The late resolution of the Quakers in Pennsylvania to set at liberty all their negro slaves, may satisfy us that their number cannot be very great. Had they made any considerable part of their property, such a resolution could never have been agreed to."[27] No mention of religious tenets, or humane motives as determining causes! The emancipation of slaves in Europe is due to nothing other than the interest of their owners and the sovereigns. Pope Alexander III issued a bull for the emancipation of the slaves, but "slavery continued to take place almost universally for

[26] *Op. cit.*, II, 289.

[27] *Ibid.*, I, 364-365. Note the evident circularity in the reasoning. The expensiveness of slave labor is the cause of its abandonment, and the abandonment is an evidence of its expensiveness.

several centuries afterwards, till it was gradually abolished by the joint operation of the two interests above mentioned, that of the proprietor on the one hand, and that of the sovereign on the other."[28]

The most striking result of the employment of the economic mode of explanation is the theory of the state as merely a union of individuals for economic ends. In its individualistic formulation this theory is not different from other political theories of the century, except that it receives a more pronounced economic coloring. Government has its origin in the inequality of fortunes among men, and is the expression of the endeavor to preserve that inequality. "Men of inferior wealth combine to defend those of superior wealth in the possession of their property, in order that men of superior wealth may combine to defend them in the possession of theirs."[29] For all purposes of the economic analysis, government remains an association of individuals for the mutual protection of their economic interests. The first rule of justice in taxation is a clear corollary: "The expense of government to the individuals of a great nation, is like the expense of management to the joint tenants of a great estate, who are all obliged to contribute in proportion to their respective interests in the estate."[30] It is equally clear that in determining the functions of the government its activities shall be confined to those things which cannot be done at all, or if so, only wastefully, by individual enterprise. The reasons for this are also economic. Governments are the greatest spendthrifts in the society, and are the least efficient means for developing particular industries. "The attention of the sovereign can be at best but a very general and vague cultivation of the greater part of his dominions." But the attention of the individual will involve a particular and minute consideration of what is likely to be the most advantageous application of his possessions in land, labor or capital.[31] Since the government is economically inefficient it receives no con-

[28] *Op. cit.*, I, 366. Cf. also other passages: I, 82; II, 181-182.
[29] *Ibid.*, II, 207. Cf. this with the *Lectures*, p. 15.
[30] *Ibid.*, II, 310.
[31] *Ibid.*, II, 318.

sideration except as an agency for preserving the conditions of free competition.

The economic order thus presented in the *Wealth of Nations* is an order in which wealth is of supreme concern and in which all the associations and activities of individuals are motivated by the economic interest. It is a consistently scientific system: every social phenomenon is explained in terms of the self-interest of individuals. Nor can there be any doubt of its logical simplicity: it has few categories, and applies them to all the facts of social life. But however logically consistent and scientifically complete the economic order which is here presented, it is undoubtedly quite different from the social order pictured in the *Moral Sentiments*. As in the *Moral Sentiments* we found the economic principles given a place, so here the question arises whether in the *Wealth of Nations* Adam Smith has recognized the other aspects of human nature presented in the moral theory.

In his scientific analysis he does not. So long as he confines himself to an explanation of the causes of individual and national wealth, he invariably employs the economic motive, as we have already demonstrated. So far as the economic analysis is concerned, the individual is always and only self-interested. There are passages in the *Wealth of Nations* which indicate another view of human nature than the purely economic one; but when they occur they are not essential to the question under discussion.

Nevertheless these occasional statements enable us to catch glimpses of a broader point of view than that with which the author is immediately concerned. The economic analysis is applied only to wealth-producing facts, and wealth for Adam Smith means material goods. But there is nowhere an implication that wealth is the only value. A factor which may be of great importance for the creation of wealth may have other effects which are not desirable. The division of labor has become a classic example of such a possibility. Adam Smith recognizes that not all has been said when the economic effects of this principle are pointed out. "The man whose whole life is spent in performing a few simple operations, of which the effects too are, perhaps, always the same, or very nearly the same, has no occasion to exert his understanding, or to exercise his invention. . . . His dexterity at his own particular trade seems, in this manner, to be acquired at the expense of his intellectual, social, and martial virtues. But in every improved and civilized society this is the state into which the laboring poor, that is, the great body of the people, must necessarily fall, unless government takes some pains to prevent it."[32] A privileged few may rise to great intellectual ability through the observation of the varied forms of activity in such a society, but "notwithstanding the great abilities of those few, all the nobler parts of the human character may be, in a great measure, obliterated and extinguished in the great body of the people." This is a clear intimation that there are other values (and those higher) than wealth. Moreover, the suggestion that government should take some means to prevent this degradation is a recognition that the state has a cultural as well as an economic purpose. "A man without the proper use of the intellectual faculties of a man, is, if possible, more contemptible than even a coward, and seems to be mutilated and deformed in a still more essential part of the character of human nature. Though the state was to derive no advantage from the instruction of the inferior ranks of people, it would still deserve its attention that they should not be altogether uninstructed."[33] But Adam Smith hastens to add that the government does in fact derive advantage from their instruction, and so remains within his economic assumptions. In these, and other passages which might be cited, we can discern a recognition that the reality goes beyond the purely economic formulation employed in the *Wealth of Nations*.[34]

In a similar way Adam Smith admits that the economic description of human nature is not true to reality. For the

[32] *Op. cit.*, II, 267-268.

[33] *Ibid.*, II, 272.

[34] Note this interesting admission: "Civil government, *so far as it is instituted for the security of property*, is in reality instituted for the defense of the rich against the poor." II, 207 (italics mine). But we have seen that the economic order regards government *only* as instituted for the security of property.

purpose of the economic analysis he consistently employs no motive except that of self-interest, yet he nowhere suggests that this is the only motive that really exists. In the explanation of prices, only the competing interests of the parties, or possible parties to the transaction are considered, yet there may frequently be other factors present. For example, rent has been explained as the result of the utmost possible greed on the part of the landlord; but "sometimes, indeed, the liberality, more frequently the ignorance, of the landlord, makes him accept of somewhat less than this portion."[35] Sometimes, also, "the ignorance of the tenant makes him undertake to pay somewhat more, or to content himself with somewhat less, than the ordinary profits of farming stock in the neighborhood." The antagonism between the interests of the merchant manufacturers and the interests of society is qualified somewhat: the merchants "are *commonly* exercised rather about the interest of their own particular branch of business, than about that of the society."[36] Self-interest again is sometimes described as being the commonest motive: "though the principles of common prudence do not always govern the conduct of every individual, they always influence that of the majority of every class or order."[37] In fact, benevolence is admitted as an actual principle at the very opening of the inquiry. "Man has almost constant occasion for the help of his brethren, and it is in vain for him to expect it from their benevolence only."[38] These passages might be indefinitely multiplied; but enough have been given to show that Adam Smith does not deny the existence of characteristics in human nature which may at times make the economic motive inoperative, or modify its operation.

There are also interesting echoes of the doctrines of sympathy in occasional passages. The disintegrating effect of city life upon the morals of a villager lies in the fact that he is deprived of the support of his neighbors' sentiments. "While he remains in a country village his conduct may be attended to, and he may be obliged to attend to it himself. In this situation and

[35] *Op. cit.*, I, 145.
[36] *Ibid.*, I, 249. Italics mine.
[37] *Ibid.*, I, 278.
[38] *Ibid.*, I, 16.

in this situation only, he may have what is called a character to lose. But as soon as he comes into a great city, he is sunk in obscurity and darkness. His conduct is observed and attended to by nobody, and he is therefore very likely to neglect it himself, and to abandon himself to every sort of low profligacy and vice."[39] The chief value of a religious sect is the mutual support which the members give to each other's morals. Again there are continual references to 'orders' of men whose interests are the same, and who act in concert as one man; but their activities, as we shall see, are economically questionable. Adam Smith admits the principle of sympathy, but can find no use for it in the economic order.

But while it is clearly evident that the explanation of the economic order rests without qualification upon the principle of self-interest, it is not quite so easy to determine what it is that Adam Smith means by self-interest. It has often been pointed out that this term, as used in the *Wealth of Nations*, seems to cover a variety of meanings. When Smith speaks of "the natural effort which every man is continually making to better his own condition," it is clearly the motive of economic gain which he has in mind. But he also calls in the aid of principles which can be differentiated from the motive of economic gain. In the celebrated chapter explaining the origin of the division of labor, the principle relied upon is the propensity to "truck, barter, and exchange one thing for another." Sometimes, again, self-interest means the impulse to activity, and sometimes the love of ease; sometimes the desire for power, and sometimes the fear of punishment. It is clearly impossible to fix upon a precise and definite psychological trait which Adam Smith considers operative in all individuals and which he relies upon to explain the economic order. It is even more impossible to interpret him as holding that the motive of economic gain, based upon rational comparison of benefits to be derived from alternative possibilities of activity, is universally—or even generally—operative. Besides ignoring the fact that the motive of economic gain is present in different degrees

[39] *Op. cit.*, II, 280.

in different individuals, such a position would also involve the assumption that the individuals in whom such an interest is operative actually know what is best for their own interests. Smith, however, would recognize that the individual seeks his own interest only as he sees it, under the limitations of his own knowledge of the relevant conditions; and his vision may be, and often is, erroneous.

We must assume a different point of view if we wish to interpret truly Adam Smith's position. It is not the motive of self-interest alone which he relies upon to explain the economic order. We have seen that competition is always associated with self-interest, and self-interest with competition; we have used the terms almost interchangeably in the above résumé of the economic reasoning, and this use which we have made merely reflects the constant substitution of the one for the other in the *Wealth of Nations*. It is self-interest *plus* competition which Adam Smith relies upon as the explanation of the economic mechanism. In other words, the really significant concept in the economic analysis is the concept of individuality, as inclusive of both self-interest and competition. Upon this conception the whole order rests. Adam Smith conceives of the economic order as purely a collection of competing individuals. The activity of each of the component individuals —whatever may be its instinctive or rational basis—is motived purely from within; but is prevented from producing consequences injurious to the common welfare by the similar internally motivated activity of other individuals.

A striking consequence of this competitive conception of the relations of individuals in society is the doctrine of wealth found in the *Wealth of Nations*—a doctrine that has become so commonly accepted in economic theory that its philosophical implications are sometimes neglected. The nation being, for the purpose of Adam Smith's inquiry, a purely economic organization, its wealth is merely the sum total of the wealth of all the individuals; and it is to be regarded as richer or poorer according to the ratio of the total consumable product to the number of competing individuals. Moreover, the wealth which is the object of the inquiry is measured in terms of *exchange values.* Although he distinguishes between value in use and value in exchange, and thus recognizes that there are many useful things that have no exchange value, Adam Smith proceeds to confine his investigation to "the principles which regulate the exchangeable value of commodities."[40] The significant result of this limitation of the economic inquiry is that he confines himself, and the science he is establishing, to a competitive definition of wealth: the economist is not concerned with those material goods which are not the objects of competition for possession. That this is not the only possible conception of political economy is strikingly shown by a work which appeared the same year as the *Wealth of Nations*—Condillac's *Le commerce et le gouvernement*—and which refuses to confine the economic inquiry to value in exchange.[41] But Adam Smith's definition of wealth as consisting only of exchangeable goods shows that he conceives of the economic order as an order of competing individuals.

Moreover, Adam Smith's position with respect to the advocacy of *laisser faire* illustrates the same point. It would seem that the practical corollary of the theoretical principles we have considered at length in this chapter would be to eliminate all governmental regulation of private enterprise, and allow the beneficent principle of self-interest to have free play; yet there are passages in the *Wealth of Nations* which recognize that the interests of certain classes are detrimental to the welfare of the whole nation. It is to the interest of the merchants and manufacturers of every country to secure to themselves the monopoly of the home market. "Their interest is, in this respect, directly opposite to that of the great body of the people."[42] "The interests of the dealers, ... in any particular branch of trade or manufactures, is always in some respects different from, and even opposite to, that of the public. . . . . The proposal of any new law or regulation of commerce which comes from this order, ought always to be listened to with great precaution, and ought never to be adopted till

[40] *Op. cit.*, I, 30.
[41] In Daire, *Collection d'Économistes*, XIV, 247 ff.
[42] *Wealth of Nations*, I, 458.

after having been long and carefully examined, not only with the most scrupulous, but with the most suspicious attention. It comes from an order of men, whose interest is never exactly the same with that of the public, who have generally an interest to deceive and even to oppress the public, and who accordingly have, upon many occasions, both deceived and oppressed it."[43] There are many such classes of which Smith, for economic reasons, was distrustful: e.g. the clergy, the laborers, the landlords, the capitalists, the merchants, "any order of men who have the smallest pretensions to independency." Each of these groups has a common interest which very often may not be identical with the interests of the nation. The reason is that individual self-interest does not receive full expression in the interests of the group. The economic mechanism can be left to work itself only if it consists of freely competing units. In other words, only in so far as the economic order of competing individuals is realized in actual society can the economic principles and their practical corollaries laid down above claim applicability.

This economic order of competing individuals needs one further qualification in order to be completely understood: Adam Smith conceives of it as the 'natural' order. As such it is both a scientific formulation of social facts on the basis of an abstract individualism, and at the same time the representation of a timeless ideal order. We have already seen that at the end of the *Moral Sentiments* Adam Smith regards the social unity as a harmonious order possessing its own laws of activity and maintenance independent of human contrivance. The *Wealth of Nations* only develops this scientific conception of society. Guided by the invisible hand, which works through the instincts of the individual, the social order creates spontaneously those institutions which are needed for the welfare of society. The *Wealth of Nations* attempts to determine these natural laws of the social order; and above all, to determine these spontaneous institutions and distinguish them from the

[43] *Op. cit.*, I, 250; cf. also I, 435; II, 282; and the examples cited by Knies, *Politische Oekonomie vom geschichtlichen Standpunkt*, pp. 224-226.

artificial contrivances of government. The practical end, therefore, of Adam Smith's inquiry is the restoration of the natural order of society by removing the artificial regulations which government has imposed. "All systems either of preference or of restraint, therefore, being thus completely taken away, the obvious and simple system of natural liberty establishes itself of its own accord."[44]

This mention of natural liberty, and the accompanying belief in a natural order, show the close connection between Adam Smith's economic theory and that of the French *Économistes.* But his indebtedness to the *Économistes* has been frequently over-estimated. That he owed much to his intercourse with the sect at Paris is not to be questioned, and the precise amount of his indebtedness has never been accurately determined.[45] It is almost certain, however, that in fundamental philosophical principles Adam Smith had nothing to learn from the Physiocrats. It was because he himself had previously worked out the conception of a social science that he was able to profit by the specific economic suggestions which his conversations with Quesnay and Turgot afforded. It seems probable that the dynamic conception of wealth as an annual product which appears in the *Wealth of Nations* is a reflection of Quesnay's *Tableau économique.* But the *Tableau* would never have produced such an impression upon Adam Smith, attempting as it did to trace the circulation and distribution of wealth in society, unless he had already arrived at the conception of a science of social phenomena. If it is necessary to find some origin for this conception in Adam Smith's thought, it could with more probability be ascribed to the influence of Montesquieu, or of his own countryman, Hume. It is going even more out of the way to attribute Adam Smith's doctrine of a natural order, and his belief in a system of natural liberty, to his contact with the French thinkers; it is far more logical to suppose that they came to him from the same source from which they came to the Physiocrats, i.e. from the political and theological ideas of Locke which dominated the century.

[44] *Op. cit.*, II, 184.

[45] Cf. the Introduction to Cannan's edition of the *Wealth of Nations*; also the introduction to the *Lectures* by the same editor.

There are also important differences between Adam Smith and the Physiocrats in their views of the natural order. The Physiocrats regarded the natural order as something to be imposed by authority, by an enlightened social physician; whereas for Smith that order is one which imposes itself, and in fact is actually to be found in existing society. He conceives of natural social laws, not so much as prescriptive in character, but rather as actual descriptions of social facts. He himself recognizes the difference between his attitude and that of the Physiocrats. "Some speculative physicians seem to have imagined that the health of the human body could be preserved only by a certain precise regimen of diet and exercise, of which every, the smallest, violation necessarily occasioned some degree of disease or disorder. . . . . Mr. Quesnai, who was himself a physician, and a very speculative physician, seems to have entertained a notion of the same kind concerning the political body, and to have imagined that it would thrive and prosper only under a certain precise regimen, the exact regimen of perfect liberty and perfect justice. He seems not to have considered that, in the political body, the natural effort which every man is continually making to better his own condition, is a principle of preservation capable of preventing and correcting, in many respects, the bad effects of a political economy, in some degree, both partial and oppressive . . . . In the political body . . . . the wisdom of nature has fortunately made ample provision for remedying many of the bad effects of the folly and injustice of man, in the same manner as it has done in the natural body, for remedying those of his sloth and intemperance."[46]

But while Adam Smith has gone farther than the Physiocrats in converting the crude form of the doctrine of natural law into a scientific and positive method of studying social facts, yet in the general presuppositions of his economic theory he has remained within the thought of his century. The employment of self-interest as the explanatory factor in the economic order represents nothing more than that he has accepted in his economic work the usual eighteenth-century

[46] *Wealth of Nations*, II, 172.

doctrine of individuality. Here it is divorced from all ethical implications because it has become the foundation of a scientific point of view. It is the conception of social relations which results from looking upon human beings from an impersonal and objective standpoint. Their differences are submerged, their inner lives of purposes and ideals are lost sight of, and they are considered merely as subject in the mass to certain general laws of activity. The philosophy of abstract individuality has become a scientific method. The acme of this abstraction is reached in Adam Smith's theory of value based upon the equality of all individuals.[47] Each human being is identical in original nature and capacities with all other human beings. "The difference between the most dissimilar characters, between a philosopher and a common street porter, for example, seems to arise not so much from nature, as from habit, custom and education."[48] The labor of all individuals is therefore homogeneous, and units of labor are as interchangeable as metal coins. "Labor . . . . is the real measure of the exchangeable value of all commodities . . . . Equal quantities of labor, at all times and places, may be said to be of equal value to the laborer."[49] It would be impossible to carry out more consistently the conclusions of an abstract logic.

The economic individualism which receives in the *Wealth of Nations* its first consistent and systematic exposition is a ripe product of eighteenth-century thought. It conceives of the social order as a system of externally related individuals, and studies their activities under the sole aspect of the production of wealth. Such an individualism is a pale and sinister reflection of the ethical and cultural individualism of the Renaissance; and the motive of self-interest which is so necessary a factor in its working is to be clearly distinguished from the factor of individual initiative which has received general recognition in modern times. The modern emphasis upon the value of individual initiative is based upon the highly dynamic doctrine of individuality which lay dormant in the Christian thought of

[47] This is only one of two inconsistent theories of value found in the *Wealth of Nations*; the other theory sets up 'cost of production' as the measure of value. Cf. Gide et Rist, *op. cit.*, pp. 88-90.

[48] *Wealth of Nations*, I, 17.

[49] *Ibid.*, I, 32, 35.

the Middle Ages and burst into full life in the period of the Renaissance and the Reformation. Owing to cultural and social circumstances resulting from the disintegration and disappearance of the medieval order, the value of individual initiative was receiving fuller recognition in practise at the beginning of the eighteenth century than ever before. The doctrine of self-interest characteristic of the seventeenth and eighteenth centuries began with the attempt to reflect in theory this practical recognition of individuality in modern life, but became entangled in a formalistic logic and ended as an abstract theory which was the very antithesis of reality. This doctrine stripped from the individual all his social qualities, abstracted him from all his human relations, and having thus dehumanized him, left him an atom in the mechanism of society, actuated necessarily by self-love. When this doctrine of naked individualism was united to the recognized truth that progress depends upon human wants and the endeavor to satisfy them, we have all the essential elements of the economic individualism as it appeared in Mandeville. And the *Wealth of Nations* is only a more elaborate, a more consistent, a more scientific and objective exposition of the same theory of society.

But the moral world? How is it related to this order of economic individualism? We have seen from the *Moral Sentiments* that the moral experience cannot be interpreted in individual or utilitarian terms; hence the moral standpoint, though recognized, is never used in the *Wealth of Nations*. The moral judgment is excluded from the scientific inquiry. As there is no recognition of benevolence so far as the working of the economic order is concerned, so there is no praise of self-seeking or self-interest. But Adam Smith does not leave these two worlds merely standing side by side. Although ethical principles have no place in the explanation of the economic order, yet the economic analysis as a whole possesses a definite relation to the standpoint of the ethical work: its point of view involves certain assumptions already recognized and criticized in the *Moral Sentiments*. What these assumptions are, from the logical standpoint, and how they affected the subsequent development of the classical economy, will have to be considered more in detail.

CHAPTER V.

Conclusion.

WHETHER or not Adam Smith can be said to have created the science of economics, as some of his admirers have claimed, it cannot be denied that the succeeding development of economic thought has been influenced predominantly by the *Wealth of Nations*. If therefore we have been able, from a study of the intellectual background of the century in which its author wrote and thought, to formulate some of the presuppositions, either latent or expressed, which lie at the base of the *Wealth of Nations*, the result has been not merely a solution of the traditional problem of relating the ethical and economic works of Adam Smith, but a suggestion toward a philosophical critique of the present-day science of economics, so far as it follows the lines laid down by him.

We have seen that the contrast between the two works of Adam Smith is the result of two divergent tendencies in eighteenth-century thought,—the one toward the employment of a traditional doctrine of abstract individualism for the scientific formulation of social laws, and the other toward an abandonment of the same individualism, and the recognition of the correlative function of individual and social factors in experience. The *Wealth of Nations* is essentially a product of the former tendency. It starts with its elements given. It assumes a society of homogeneous human units, and attempts to formulate the laws of their activities in the production of wealth. The economic order is therefore a perfectly adjusted mechanism, in which each part instinctively but efficiently serves the ends of the whole. But the *Moral Sentiments* shows its close relation to the contrasting current of ethical thought by questioning the individualistic starting point. Instead of taking the individual as 'given' and moved only by a single impulse, it examines the facts of his experience and finds that he is social through and through. It is because he is the product of society that his acts conform to the social welfare. His very interests are those which have been instilled into him by his social environment, and hence in pursuing his own interests he is also pursuing those of his society. The rigid distinction between self and others is seen to break down. The very reason why the individual desires to advance his own welfare is because he wishes the approval and admiration of his fellowmen;[1] so that even the motive of self-interest is not individual but social in its origin. The *Moral Sentiments* shows the inner organic relation which exists between all the individuals of a society and the social unity.

The very evident contrast between the two points of view represented in the economic and the ethical theories makes all the more significant the distinction which is found in the *Moral Sentiments* between the lower, mechanical interpretation of society—the plane of justice—and the higher, benevolent point of view. The interadaptation of the parts and the whole in the social unity is manifested upon two different planes of activity, as we have seen in our analysis of the *Moral Sentiments:* first, upon the plane of instincts, and later upon the plane of reflective consciousness. In the first instance, the society is an unconscious unity. The individuals are instinctively serving each other's purposes, and serving them efficiently. In the second instance, the individual has through sympathy become conscious of his organic relation to the social whole; he sees its ends, and the ends of other individuals, as his own. This is the stage whereon the strictly moral experience appears; the individual here judges his actions from the standpoint of the impartial spectator, that is, from the social viewpoint. Now the limited character of the economic work is not that it confines itself to a separate economic world where ethical relations play no part, but that it deals with human activity in mechanical terms. The 'economic man' is an individual who acts purely as an individual, without explicit recognition of his social relationship. This plane of activity is the necessary foundation for all the higher life of the individual, but it is not

[1] *Moral Sentiments*, pt. iv, ch. 1.

that which constitutes the excellence of human nature, and hence the conception of society which considers individuals as only thus mechanically related cannot be said to have grasped the most significant elements in the social experience.

If our interpretation of the contrast between justice and benevolence is correct, we are justified in concluding that for Adam Smith the economic analysis, as corresponding to the plane of justice, is admittedly an inadequate representation of the social order. Besides our interpretation of this ethical dualism, however, there are other grounds which support the same conclusion. We have only to recall once more the place of political economy in Adam Smith's scheme of moral philosophy. As a part of the lectures on jurisprudence, the economic analysis deals with social facts under one aspect only, that of their relation to the production of wealth; and it explains them on a basis of abstract individualism which Adam Smith has left behind in his ethical work. In these two respects, then, the economic analysis falls short of the concrete theory of social and moral relations developed in the *Moral Sentiments*. Nor does the *Wealth of Nations* itself fail to recognize these limitations. Since the economic theory deals only with the material aspect of human life, it is clearly a technological inquiry and subordinate to a philosophy of values: if the increase of national wealth is the end desired, then the economic theory can point out the means. But whether this end itself is as valuable as other possible ends, the economic theory does not answer; and the *Wealth of Nations* recognizes, as we have seen, not only that there are other and higher values than wealth, but also that the pursuit of wealth often threatens the destruction of these higher values. Moreover, the *Wealth of Nations* does not fail to recognize that the abstract order of isolated individuals is not a true picture of human society. Instead of consisting of identical units acting upon one another only through self-interest, society is composed of individuals who belong to various groups, and whose sentiments and interests are moulded by those groups. It is on these grounds that, as we have seen, the author refuses to advocate unlimited *laisser faire*. This refusal is plainly a recognition that society is not really so individualistic as his theory assumes. In the natural order there would be little need of government interference, for each individual would promote the public welfare in seeking his own advantage; but in the actual social order there are associations of individuals which would seek to impose their class interests upon the country to the detriment of the national prosperity. Adam Smith distinctly recognizes the limited validity of his individualistic economics.

Nevertheless, there were circumstances of a historical and practical character, both during Adam Smith's lifetime and later, which tended to emphasize this economic individualism at the expense of the ethical theory. The individualistic assumptions were characteristic of the thought of the eighteenth century, and we have seen that the unique importance of the *Theory of Moral Sentiments* is to be found in the fact that it showed their inadequacy in the moral experience. After 1763, when Adam Smith resigned his professorship at Glasgow, there is no reason to suppose that he occupied himself for any length of time with ethical questions. The additions made to later editions of the *Moral Sentiments* show no development from the position expounded in 1759. At the same time his already keen interest in economics was increased by his contact with the French *Économistes*, and in the elaboration of his class-room lectures that interest induced him to depart from the regular order, which would have suggested that he publish first the section relating to Jurisprudence. The second half of the century was a period of intense activity in economic thought; and to the developing political economy the concept of individualism was thoroughly adapted. It is altogether probable, therefore, that in the development of the *Wealth of Nations* Adam Smith simply followed the current of his times and ceased to speculate along the more concrete lines laid down in the *Moral Sentiments*. The full meaning of his own doctrine of sympathy was probably not apparent even to himself; its importance is appreciable only at this distance of time, and in the light of the intervening development of thought. In any case, Adam Smith followed the usual course and made the individualism of the doctrine of natural law the basis of his political economy.

But the main import of the individualism of the *Wealth of Nations* is perhaps to be found in another connection. The doctrine of natural law from which it was derived was not only a philosophy of natural jurisprudence, but a philosophy of the rights of man. The explosive force which it contained became manifest in the revolutionary principles of the latter half of the century. Adam Smith's connection with this revolutionary philosophy cannot be ignored. We have already noticed that he broke with the Physiocratic thought in asserting the natural equality of all men, and based on this belief his theory of labor value. Rousseau's essay on the *Origin and Foundations of Inequality among Men* had early attracted his attention, and his review of this work contained in an article in the *Edinburgh Review* of 1755 showed a significant suspension of judgment: he seemed to be waiting for further development of Rousseau's thought before determining his attitude toward it.[2] There can be no doubt that he followed the progress of the revolutionary philosophy with great interest. When he ascribed the origin of government to the rise of private property he probably showed the influence of the above-mentioned essay of Rousseau. Another point of agreement with Rousseau was his distrust of class interests in government, and his belief that the general welfare is best expressed by individuals, not by groups. Consequently, though we have every reason to believe that Adam Smith's political attitude was never very sympathetic toward the revolutionary philosophy, yet his economic theory came very near the revolutionary spirit in its advocacy of measures for the liberation of the individual. Here his scientific use of abstract individualism was converted into a practical program. The actual order must be transformed in accordance with the individualistic doctrine of natural liberty. Collective action was, so far as possible, to give way to the free competition of individuals; and this state of free competition was the natural, reasonable and beneficent order. The *Wealth of Nations* was therefore an application to economic questions of the same ideal of liberating the individual which found expression in the *Social Contract* and *Émile*.

[2] Delatour, *Adam Smith*, p. 84.

The liberalizing purpose of the *Wealth of Nations* involves without doubt a divergence from the *Moral Sentiments*. But the divergence thus introduced in theoretical outlook is largely based upon the recognition of the practical necessity of combating certain abuses of collective activity. The emphasis upon, and seeming laudation of self-interest in the *Wealth of Nations* is to be regarded as primarily a revolt against the undue interference of the state in economic affairs, of which Adam Smith had seen so many examples in France and in his own country. As a corrective of over-regulation, the doctrine of individual freedom was legitimate; as a corrective of the tendency to submerge the individual in groups no longer useful, the doctrine of self-interest was necessary. It is probable that neither of these doctrines apart from the propagandist context would have been stated so positively. The theoretical doctrine of the relation of the individual to his social environment given in the *Moral Sentiments* is not to be regarded as abandoned.

Such was the theoretical and historical basis of the *Wealth of Nations*, and such were the economic traditions which the classical economists inherited from Adam Smith. For better or worse, the "older economy" was historically conditioned by the individualistic period in which it arose; it was a typical product of eighteenth-century rationalism. The doctrine of individualism became more prominent as the classical economy developed in the hands of Ricardo, Senior and Mill. Upon the assumption of a society of freely competing individuals, Ricardo discovered a compact system of economic laws, as exact and uniform as natural laws in the physical world; but there was no explicit recognition of their abstract character. Senior cited self-interest as one of the universally admitted principles upon which the theoretic part of economics is based; and asserted that the natural order of freely competing individuals is in general true to reality.[3] Mill showed the same individualistic viewpoint; he recognized for the first time the deductive character of the classical economics, and the provi-

[3] *Introductory Lecture*, pp. 7, 30.

sional validity of its conclusions; and he urged that the premises be extended beyond the limited few which had hitherto served as the basis of the science. But he did not call in question the individualistic method: social laws are nothing but the generalizations of the acts of individuals in society; they are to be ascertained by the method of Composition of Causes, and the data of explanation are to be found in the facts of human (i.e. individual) nature.[4] After Mill the classical doctrines were temporarily thrust into the background by antagonistic tendencies—dissatisfaction with *laisser faire*, the rise of the Historical School, and socialistic theories of various kinds. These anti-individualistic tendencies did not long prevail. The classical method has been revived in the last quarter of the nineteenth century and made even more rigid in its character by the application of mathematics. The attempt is made to find the mathematical statement for the laws governing the interaction of individuals, considered simply as self-interested atoms in the economic mechanism. Both this school and the psychological school, which represent to-day the most vigorous movements in economic thought, derive their abstract method and their individualistic conception of society by direct line from the economic theory of Adam Smith. The only important change in viewpoint is that in the hands of the later economists the abstract character of the science and the methodological purpose of the assumptions have become explicit. The science of economics was founded in an age of individualism, and in general it has remained true to its initial conception.

It cannot indeed be denied that the Historical School which arose with Roscher and Knies in opposition to certain tendencies in the older economy was justified in appealing to Adam Smith as having employed the historical method. There is a very decided element of historical inquiry in the *Wealth of Nations*; Adam Smith uses both the inductive-historical, and the abstract-deductive methods—only for him the sharp differentiation between the two methods did not exist. In

[4] *Logic*, bk. vi, chs. 7, 8, 9.

any case the conclusions of the Historical School have not after all seriously differed from those of the classical economy, so far as the formulation of laws for present economic societies is concerned. Their main achievement is having made explicit the necessity of assumptions in a general science such as economics professes to be, and having shown that the assumptions of the classical economy are based upon the actual historical and economic situation of modern European societies, and that they would be useless in attempting to deal with other societies possessing a different social organization. But the possession of both these characteristics is a proof of soundness rather than of weakness in the science attacked, and the failure of the Historical School to provide anything more than contributions to economic history proves indirectly the inherent sureness of the course upon which economics has since the time of Adam Smith been embarked.

Political economy, therefore, has followed, not only in its general subject-matter, but also in its method and philosophical presuppositions, the tradition which Adam Smith established by the *Wealth of Nations*. It is founded upon the individualism of the doctrine of natural law and natural rights which dominated the thought of the eighteenth century and has continued to form the basis of most of our present political and legal institutions. Its stronghold is the absolute character of individuality, which is the common starting-point of our legal and religious codes, as well as of unreflective thinking. In reducing the facts of social experience to purely individual acts, and in regarding the acts of all individuals merely in their wealth-getting aspect, it has been able to formulate a mechanics of social life. This cannot by any means be regarded as an invalid procedure. If the economist chooses to consider only one aspect of human activity with the purpose of contributing to the interpretation of the whole of concrete experience, there can be no logical objection. It must be recognized, however, that the mechanics of social life which the economic analysis exhibits is not all there is in social experience. For the economist, wealth is the end of activity, but in concrete experience it is only one of many ends.

For the economist, every action is merely individual; but human activity is also universal as well as particular. Because of these two initial assumptions, which belong to the very nature of his science, the economist—*qua* economist—can never grasp the full meaning of social experience.

The limitations of economic theory are easily evident to-day to anyone who will take the time to reflect upon its presuppositions. The work of the last half of the nineteenth century in investigating and clarifying the problems of scientific method has carried us beyond the point where we are likely to confuse a scientific construction with the concrete reality of experience. But it was not so easy to formulate this distinction in Adam Smith's day. The classical economy, especially in its young and vigorous days, was disposed to assume to itself a competence to solve all problems; and it cannot be said that Adam Smith entirely escaped this danger. Nevertheless in abandoning the current individualism as inadequate to express the highest and most significant aspects of the moral experience, and in recognizing that the mechanical relation of an individual to his economic order is only the external form of the inner relation which he bears to the whole of his social environment, Adam Smith has anticipated and suggested a solution to one of the most important of present-day problems.